FOLK SONGS FROM NEWFOUNDLAND

Collected and edited

by

MAUD KARPELES

FABER AND FABER

London

First published in 1971
by Faber and Faber Limited
3 Queen Square London WC1
Printed in Great Britain by
Latimer Trend & Co Ltd Plymouth
All rights reserved

ISBN 0 571 09297 7

To
the memory
of
MARIUS BARBEAU

CONTENTS

9

CONTENTS

CONTENTS

CONTENTS

DANCES

APPENDIX

Texts Adapted for Singing

INTRODUCTION

This collection of 150 tunes has been selected from a total of 191 noted in Newfoundland during two expeditions made in September and October, 1929, and in July and August, 1930, each lasting about seven weeks.

I had long had such a collecting expedition in mind and I had hoped it would have been in Cecil Sharp's company. We had, in fact, planned to go to Newfoundland in 1918 after our final expedition to the Southern Appalachian Mountains, but we were prevented by lack of funds. Again, we made preparations to go in 1925, but Cecil Sharp's untimely death in June 1924 intervened. Ultimately, I decided to make the expedition by myself. I did so with some trepidation as I had had little previous experience of noting tunes, and the tape-recorder had not then come into use.

I set out with two introductions in my pocket and very little idea of what folk songs, if any, I should find. At that time, in contrast to the present day, there were comparatively few published collections of folk songs from North America and it was not realized that folk songs of English origin had survived throughout a wide area. I believed Newfoundland to be virgin, if not barren, soil. In this I was mistaken, as I discovered soon after my arrival, for the Vassar College Folklore Expedition,[1] consisting of Mrs. Greenleaf and Mrs. Grace Yarrow Mansfield (then Miss Yarrow) had preceded me by two months. In fact, Mrs. Greenleaf had even noted some songs nine years earlier when she had worked with Dr. Wilfred Grenfell's Mission as a school teacher. However, my tracks only crossed those of the Vassar Expedition at one point—at Fortune Harbour, Notre Dame Bay.

Newfoundland, which became the tenth Province of Canada in 1949, had previously prided itself on being Great Britain's oldest colony. It was probably known to the Norsemen as early as the beginning of the eleventh century A.D. Nearly four hundred years later, in 1497,[2] it was discovered by John Cabot, and Henry VII gave 'to him that found the

[1] See Greenleaf and Mansfield, *Ballads and Sea Songs of Newfoundland*, Harvard University Press, 1933.

[2] It is probable that Bristol men fished off the Newfoundland coast at a slightly earlier date.

13

new isle £10'. From then on English ships as well as those of other nations visited the island for the sake of the fishing. It was not, however, until 1583 that Sir Humphrey Gilbert, having set sail from Plymouth with five ships and a crew of two hundred and sixty men, took formal possession of the island in the name of Queen Elizabeth. Incidentally, one may note that he took with him besides a variety of music, 'morris dancers, hobby horse and May-like conceits to delight the savage people'. Sir Humphrey Gilbert stayed in Newfoundland only seventeen days and was shipwrecked and drowned on the voyage home.

The first real attempt at settlement was made in 1610 when a Royal Charter was granted to the 'Treasurer and the Company of Adventurers and Planters of the City of London and Bristol for the Colony or Plantations in Newfoundland' and John Guy was appointed the first Governor. This was the prelude to bitter disputes, which raged for about two hundred years, between the settlers and the visiting fishermen: disputes in which the rights of the settlers received but little recognition from the Mother Country. Another trouble which beset the Colony in its early days and often led to fierce fighting was the rivalry of the fishermen of other lands, particularly Portuguese, Spanish, French, Basque and Dutch. French colonization began in 1662 and up to the end of the eighteenth century there were intermittent duels between the French and the English which accounted for much loss of life. The islands of St. Pierre and Miquelon are still French territory.[1]

Until the end of the seventeenth century there was only a small resident population, the majority of fishermen returning to England each year. But throughout the eighteenth century there was a big increase in the number of permanent residents, particularly of those coming from Ireland; and again in the early nineteenth century there was a big influx of immigrants from the south of Ireland. Today, the great majority of the people are of English and Irish descent: those from England coming mainly from the south-west counties of Somerset, Dorset, Devon and Cornwall.

It has been said that 'there is no civilized nation in the world which is so marine in its character as Newfoundland. The sea has asserted its sway over Newfoundlanders; they are wedded with the sea and "their children's eyes change colour with the sea". Cod, seals, herrings, whales and the clownish lobsters mould their destiny.'[2] There are at the present time a number of mines in operation as well as pulp and paper mills. Otherwise the main industry now as in the past is fishing.

[1] For songs of French origin surviving in these islands, see Carmen Roy, *Saint Pierre et Miquelon*, Musée National du Canada, Bulletin No. 182.
[2] J. D. Rogers, *A Historical Geography of the British Colonies*, Vol. V, Part iv, 'Newfoundland', Oxford, 1911; pp. 236–7.

INTRODUCTION

Except for St. John's and Corner Brook there were few towns of any size and the majority of the people lived in small settlements, or 'outports' as they are called, which are dotted along the shores of the mainland or on the islands.

The scenery, with its great sweeping bays and land-locked harbours which give the appearance of lakes, is of surpassing beauty. As in Norway there are high cliffs going sheer down to the water. These are sometimes bare and rugged and at other times wooded right to the water's edge. In the early summer the ground is carpeted with blue irises and rhodora and in the autumn when the blueberry leaves have turned there is a blaze of colour. The interior consists of big lakes, rivers, virgin forests and moorland—'barrens'—and was mostly uninhabited. There was no agriculture on any extensive scale, but each family in the outports grew potatoes and vegetables for its own consumption and will often keep goats, sheep and a cow.

The coastline of Newfoundland is very irregular. The great island-studded bays and narrower inlets often penetrate the land to a great depth, cutting it up into a series of peninsulas. Thus it is, or was, a very difficult country to get about in. On the peninsula of Avalon, where forty per cent of the population lived, there were roads which connected St. John's to most of the outports on the peninsula, and there were small local roads in other parts of the island, but at the time I was there, there were no through roads linking one peninsula to another. A railway traversed the island, running north from St. John's to Notre Dame Bay, then turning westward to the coast and finally southward to Port-aux-Basques, the port for North Sydney on Cape Breton Island. This main railway, with its three-day-a-week service, had a few branch lines, but connections were usually inconvenient, so that much precious time had to be spent in travelling.

The majority of outports could only be reached by boat. There were the mail-steamers which ply the coast, calling once a week or once a fortnight at the more important settlements, and the local services of bay boats, which link the port served by the branch railway with other ports in the bay; but to get to many of the settlements one had to charter an open motor-boat.

Owing to the shortness of my sojourn and the difficulties of travel, my itinerary needed careful planning and it was often difficult to decide whether to take advantage of a passing steamer before the settlement had been fully explored, or to risk being stranded empty-handed for several days.

It was, of course, only possible to prospect a very small part of the country. I visited some forty outports and noted songs from 104 singers. In 1929 my main centres of exploration were Conception Bay and

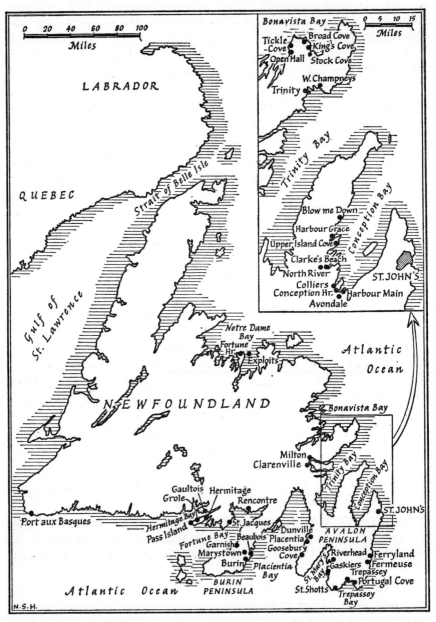

Map of Newfoundland showing outports where songs were collected

INTRODUCTION

Bonavista Bay on the east coast and I also made short visits to Trinity Bay and Notre Dame Bay. In 1930 I concentrated on the south coast, the main centres being Placentia Bay, Fortune Bay and Hermitage Bay, and in addition, I got a few songs from St. Mary's Bay, and Trepassey Bay.

I had hoped that Newfoundland might yield a wealth of songs comparable with the riches that Cecil Sharp and I had discovered in the Southern Appalachian Mountains a decade earlier. The original settlement of Newfoundland is as old as, if not older than that of the Appalachian Mountains, but the island has not had the same immunity from modern civilization, for the sea does not isolate to the same extent as does a mountain range. Consequently, folk songs were not so easily found as in the Appalachians. There, old and young knew them and sang but little else; in Newfoundland the 'old' songs were fast going out of fashion. Generally speaking, few of the young people had learned them and the old people had often to search their memories in order to recall them. In fact, the state of folk song in Newfoundland was probably not very different from what it had been in England at the turn of the century.

The people from whom I gathered the songs were nearly all fisherfolk. My quest seemed a strange one to them, particularly when I had disposed of the idea that I was on the stage or the agent of a gramophone company. They were convinced that I should make a lot of money out of the songs. 'If I could do that, I should never have to do another day's fishing', said one singer after I had noted down his song and sung it back to him. However, they did not grudge me my supposed reward or even expect to share it. Once they realized that their songs were appreciated, they were always ready to sing and they would go out of their way to help me to find songs. One day when I was crossing a bay by motor-boat, my navigator spent his time studiously writing out songs on scraps of paper. At intervals throughout our journey he shyly handed me the results of his labour asking if they would be of any use to me.

Indeed, it would be impossible to find a kindlier or friendlier people than the Newfoundlanders. Wherever I went I was instantly welcome, although I came as a complete stranger without introduction. Everyone was delighted to meet 'that girl from England' and to hear what the people 'at home' were doing and thinking.

Crime in the outports was unknown and the only danger in walking along a lonely road after dark might be a chance encounter with ghosts or fairies. This prospect did not alarm me, but I had a wholesome fear of the dogs that prowled around every dwelling.

In Newfoundland, as in other parts of the world, singers do not distinguish between traditional and composed songs, and many is the time that I have tracked down a singer with a reputation for old songs only to be regaled with 'When you and I were Young, Maggie', or 'The Letter edged with Black'. In order to convey what I wanted, I used sometimes to explain that I was looking for songs that had not been put into books or that had no 'music' to them, which to the folk singer means the printed air. I was once caught out by this ruse: a singer, coming to the end of his repertory of composed popular songs, all of which I had rejected on the grounds that they were already in print, innocently remarked: 'Well, I can only think that some other young lady must have come along before you and got all the songs printed off'.

The proportion of authentic folk songs is small compared with the general repertory. In addition to the composed songs of an earlier generation, songs are constantly being made up about contemporary events such as exploits at sea, shipwrecks, etc. These are often set to a well-known 'Come-all-ye' type of tune. They usually have but little aesthetic value and since my interest lay in songs that represent an older tradition I did not note any of them.[1]

It will be seen from the Notes that most of the songs in this collection stem from the British Isles and that they are also known in other regions of the North American Continent, more particularly in Nova Scotia. In many cases there is a very close resemblance both in tune and text between the versions[2] noted in Newfoundland and in England.

The proportion of modal tunes appears to be higher than in England. Of the 150 tunes in this collection 69 are modal, or 87 if we include those in which the seventh is absent or variable. They can be thus analysed:

With Minor Third

Dorian	24
No sixth	24
Aeolian	7
	— 55

With Major Third

Mixolydian	14
No seventh	13
Variable seventh	5
	— 32
	87

About 52 per cent of the tunes have the common structural arrange-

[1] A number of such songs will be found in Greenleaf and Mansfield, op. cit., and in Gerald Doyle's *Old-Time Songs of Newfoundland*, St. John's, 1927; 3rd ed. 1955.

[2] It should be noted that the term 'version' has been used as synonymous with 'variant' regardless of the extent of the variation between the sets of the tune or the text.

ment of four varying phrases: A B C D. The second largest category—about 26 per cent (or 30 per cent if the unpublished tunes are included) —have the A B B A formula, in which the B phrase usually finishes on the dominant and the A phrase on the tonic which is twice repeated in the fourth and final phrase. One is tempted to think that this form is of Irish origin, but proof of this hypothesis would need a good deal of further research. Certainly, it is far commoner in songs noted in Ireland than in those noted in England. It seems to appear more commonly in Anglo-Irish songs, i.e. songs in the English language, than in the Gaelic songs. The thesis that the formula is characteristic of Irish folk music is supported by Phillips Barry[1] who for convenience described it as the 'Come-all-ye' type of tune. He comments on its artificiality and he suggests that it may be a survival of an early artistic convention in folk music. Cecil Sharp,[2] on the other hand, observes that the formula is quite a common one in English folk tunes. He quotes 'The Banks of the Sweet Dundee' (of which 'Down by a Riverside', No. 65 in this collection, is a variant) as the 'stock-in-trade of every English folk singer' and the tune that he will most readily produce when memory fails him. This is true enough and, moreover, the attraction of this tune is so great that once a folk singer has it in mind he will find it hard to get rid of and will be apt to sing all subsequent songs to the same tune. It is perhaps of interest to note that the form occurs but rarely in the older ballads in this collection. In the Child Ballads there are only four instances: Nos. 6A, 6B and 20 with the second and fourth phrases ending on the dominant, and No. 24 with the second and fourth phrases ending on the sub-dominant.

One agrees with Phillips Barry with regard to the artificiality of this form and one might add that it shows a certain lack of invention. However, despite the prevalence of this 'Come-all-ye' type of tune, which makes for monotony, the general standard of the tunes is high. They are mostly types that are familiar to us from other collections, but many of them have an individual beauty which sets them apart: such are 'Sweet William's Ghost', 'The Maiden's Lament' and 'She's like the Swallow', to mention only a few.

A characteristic of some of the singers was a seeming inability or reluctance to strike the tune straight away. In the first few stanzas the tune was quite indeterminate and it crystallized only as the song proceeded. Many singers introduced variants in the successive stanzas, but I was rarely able to capture these and had to content myself with noting the skeleton of the tune.

In my notations I have placed the tunes in a key which fits con-

[1] *British Ballads from Maine*, p. xxviii, Yale University Press, 1923.
[2] *English Folk Songs: Some Conclusions*, pp. 74–5, Heinemann, 1965.

INTRODUCTION

veniently into the staff. The singers' choice of pitch was more or less fortuitous and I have not therefore considered it necessary to indicate it.

The songs have been grouped roughly according to subject matter. This arrangement is less for the purpose of classification than as a means of helping to locate the songs; for, in the absence of standard titles, apart from the Child Ballads, their identity is not always immediately obvious. The system adopted is not altogether consistent. For instance, the Child Ballads which take pride of place have been grouped together irrespective of subject matter; and the third category, Ballads and Narrative Songs, is somewhat heterogeneous, containing partly ballads which seem to have some affinity with the Child Ballads in what one might call their classical mode of expression, and partly ballads which do not fit into any particular category. Then again, a few of the songs might well be placed under more than one heading.

Although many of the texts have been preserved in a more or less complete and coherent form, there are some that have been mutilated owing to lack of memory and other causes. For those who wish to sing the songs, and not merely to study them, there is given in the Appendix a few composite versions of the text and suggestions for amending some of the faulty lines. In the Notes on the songs other versions have occasionally been quoted for the sake of comparison and a possible explanation has been given of a few obscure words and phrases.

If one looks at this collection as a whole, one's feeling of wonder at the persistence of tradition is renewed. The singer of 'Lord Bateman' expressed to his wife his astonishment that a stranger should be so much like themselves; but in listening to the familiar story of the 'noble lord' and his 'young Sophia' together with the 'proud young porter' and the bride's mother who was 'never heard to speak so free', it was hard for the stranger to recall that two thousand miles of ocean lay between Newfoundland and Somerset.

In conclusion I would thank all those who have helped me and in particular my friends, Mr. and Mrs. Fred Emerson, who offered me generous hospitality in their home at St. John's and gave me much valuable information. I would also acknowledge my gratitude to the singers who so patiently sang for me. I hope that this publication will help to restore to them their confidence in the value and beauty of the songs which they and their forefathers have treasured and which have in the past afforded so much pleasure.

Finally, I would place on record my appreciation of the generous assistance which the Provincial Government of Newfoundland and the Canadian Folk Music Society have given towards the publication of this book.

London, 1970   MAUD KARPELES

BALLADS AND SONGS

Child Ballads

1 THE OUTLANDISH KNIGHT
(Lady Isabel and the Elf Knight)

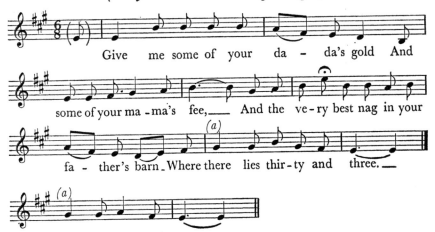

Give me some of your dada's gold
And some of your mamma's fee,
And the very best nag in your father's barn
Where there lies thirty and three.

So he rode then along, along,
Till he came to a river-side.
Alight, alight, says he;
Six fair maids I have a-drowned here
And you the seventh shall be.

Six fair pretty maids you have a-drowned here
And why do you do so by me?
You promised you'd marry me when you came to Green Fields
And both would married be.

Take off your rich, your costly robe
And lay it down by me,
For it is too rich and too costly
To rot in the salt sea.

O turn, O turn, young Willie, she says,
O turn your back to me.
Pretty Polly she took him all into her arms
And throwed him into the sea.

23

Lie there, lie there, false Willie, she says,
Lie there instead of me.
You thought you'd strip me as I was born,
Not one lack [?] did I take from thee.

And then she mounted her meelyer [*sic*] bright
And faced the green apple tree.
She rode along, along and along
This long summer's day.

She rode till she came to her father's hall,
Hearing what the parrot did say:
Where were you, my pretty Polly,
This livelong summer's day?

O hush, O hush, pretty Polly, she says,
Don't tell no tales of me.
Your cage shall be made of the glittering gold
And your door of ivory.

Her father was in the very next room
Hearing what the parrot did say.
What is the matter with pretty Polly,
She chatters so long before day.

Those cats are coming against my cage-door
Trying to make war against me,
And I am calling for pretty Polly
To drive those cats away.

Sung by Mr. Matthew Aylward at Stock Cove, Bonavista Bay, 20th
September 1929

2 EARL BRAND

Arise, arise, King Henry, he said. Or
are you not at home? A - rise and take care of your
youngest daughter dear, For the el - dest are go - ing with me.

Arise, arise, King Henry, he said,
Or are you not at home?
Arise and take care of your youngest daughter dear,
For the eldest are going with me.

Arise, arise, my seven sons bold,
And put on your armour so bright,
It never shall be said that daughter of mine
Shall be married to a lord or a knight.

Arise, arise, Lady Margaret, he said,
And hold the white steed in your hand,
While I go and fight with your seven brothers bold
And your father in the meadow where he stands.

Lady Margaret she rose and held the white steed,
She stood and never shed a tear
Until she had seen her seven brothers fall
And her father that loved her so dear.

Ease your hand, ease your hand, Lord Robert, she cries,
For your blows they are wonderful sore,
Sweethearts I may get, many's the one,
But a father dear I never will get more.

Choose your choice, choose your choice, Lady Margaret, he says,
Will you come along with me for a bride?
I must go along with you, Lord Robert, she said,
For you've left me without any guide.

Lord Robert he mounted on a milk-white steed,
And she on a dapple grey.
He went sounding of his bugle both loud and shrill
And went bleeding along the highway.

He bled till he came to his own mother's door,
How loud he did rap at the ring.
Open the door, dear mother, he cries,
You know my fair lady I have won.

Make my bed both deep and wide,
O make it wide and deep
And lay Lady Margaret down by my side,
May the sounder or the better I may sleep.

Lord Robert he died about midnight,
Lady Margaret she died before day.
I hope every couple that may now be together
May find more enjoyment than they.

Sung by Thomas Ghaney (72) at Colliers, Conception Bay, 22nd October 1929

3 THE BONNY BANKS OF VIRGIE-O
(*Babylon*)

A

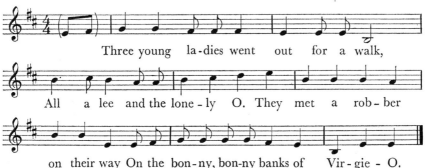

Three young la-dies went out for a walk,
All a lee and the lone-ly O. They met a rob-ber
on their way On the bon-ny, bon-ny banks of Vir-gie-O.

Three young ladies went out for a walk,
  All a lee and the lonely O.
They met a robber on their way
  On the bonny, bonny banks of Virgie-O.

He took the first one by the hand,
And whipped her around till he made her stand.

O will you be a robber's wife,
Or will you die by my penknife?

I will not be a robber's wife;
I would rather die by your penknife.

He took the penknife in his hand,
And it's there he took her own sweet life.

He took the second one by the hand,
And whipped her around till he made her stand.

As in stanzas 3, 4 and 5.

He took the third one by the hand,
And whipped her around till he made her stand.

O will you be a robber's wife,
Or will you die by my penknife?

I will not be a robber's wife,
Nor I will not die by your penknife.

If my brothers were here tonight,
You would not have killed my sisters fair [*or* bright].

Where are your brothers, pray now tell?
One of them is a minister.

And where is the other, I pray now tell?
He's out a-robbing like yourself.

The Lord have mercy on my poor soul,
I've killed my sisters all but one.

Then he took his penknife in his hand,
And then he took away his own sweet life.

Sung by Mr. and Mrs. Kenneth Monks at Kings Cove, Bonavista Bay, 24th
September 1929

B

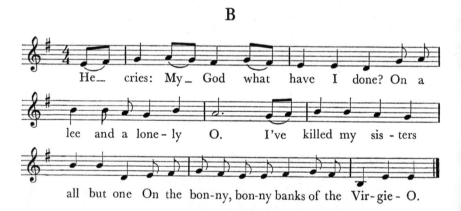

He— cries: My— God what have I done? On a
lee and a lone-ly O. I've killed my sis-ters
all but one On the bon-ny, bon-ny banks of the Vir-gie- O.

Sung by Miss Florrie Snow (15) at North River, Conception Bay, 17th
October 1929

THE BONNY BANKS OF VIRGIE-O

C

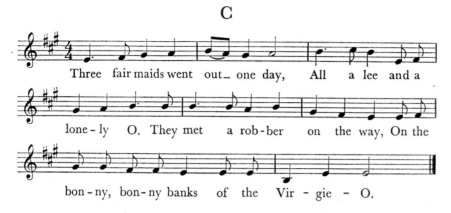

Three fair maids went out— one day, All a lee and a lone-ly O. They met a rob-ber on the way, On the bon-ny, bon-ny banks of the Vir - gie - O.

Sung by Mrs. Bridget (Robt.) Hall at North River, Conception Bay, 16th October 1929

D

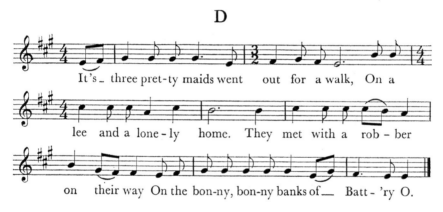

It's— three pret-ty maids went out for a walk, On a lee and a lone-ly home. They met with a rob-ber on their way On the bon-ny, bon-ny banks of— Batt- 'ry O.

Sung by Mrs. May Ellen Snow at North River, Conception Bay, 16th October 1929

4 HIND HORN
OR
THE BEGGAR MAN
A

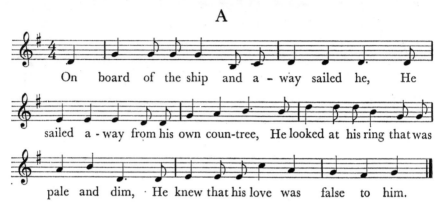

On board of the ship and away sailed he,
He sailed away from his own countree,
He looked at his ring that was pale and dim,
He knew that his love was false to him.

On board of the ship and back sailed he,
He sailed right back to his own countree,
He looked at his ring and it was pale and dim,
And he knew that his love was false to him.

He rode and he rode and he rode up the street,
An old beggarman he chanced to meet.
What news, what news have you got for me?
Tomorrow is your true love's wedding-day
And the squire is invited to give her away.

You haul off your begging rig
And I'll take off my driving suit.
The begging rig it won't fit me,
Your driving suit it won't fit thee.

But let it be right or let it be wrong,
The beggar's suit he did put on.
He rode till he came to Napoleon's gate,
And he lay on his staff in a weary state.

He saw his true love tripping down the stairs,
Gold rings on her fingers and gold in her hair,

HIND HORN or THE BEGGAR MAN

And in her hand a glass of wine
All for to treat the old beggarman.

He drank and he drank and he drank so free
And into the glass the ring slipped he.
Did you get it by land, did you get it by strand,
Or did you get it from a drowned man's hand?

I neither got it from the land, I neither got it from the strand,
Nor neither did I get it from a drowned man's hand,
But I got it from your true love was courting you so free,
And now I'm returned on your wedding day.

Then the gold from her fingers she then hauled off
And the gold from her hair it did fall off,
I will follow my true love for ever, ever more
And beg my bread from door to door.

Between the kitchen and the hall
The old beggar's suit he did let fall.
He showed his true love the flower of them all,
He's the nicest little fellow that stands in the hall.

Sung by Mr. Joseph Quann at Rencontre, Fortune Bay, 18th July 1930

B

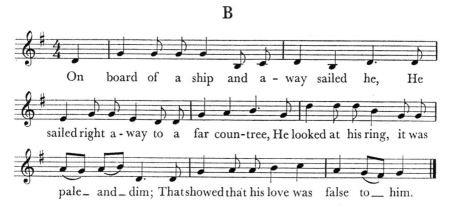

On board of a ship and a-way sailed he, He
sailed right a-way to a far coun-tree, He looked at his ring, it was
pale— and— dim; That showed that his love was false to— him.

Sung by Mr. Jacob Courage at Frenchman's Cove, Garnish, Fortune Bay,
15th July 1930

5 THE CRUEL MOTHER

A

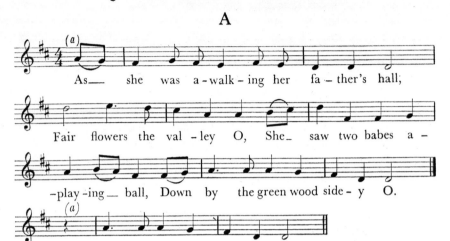

As she was a-walking her father's hall,
    Fair flowers the valley O,
She saw two babes a-playing ball,
    Down by the greenwood sidey O.

She says: Dear babes, if you were mine,
I would dress you up in silk so fine.

O, they said, dear mother, when we were yours,
You neither dressed us in silk or coarse.

You took a penknife from your skirt,
And you pierced it in our tender hearts.

THE CRUEL MOTHER

She said: Dear babes, it's you can tell,
If my poor soul is for heaven or hell.

Yes, dear mother, we can tell
Whether your poor soul's for heaven or hell.

You have seven years to roll a stone,
Seven more to stand alone,
And the rest of your time you'll walk alone,
    Down by the greenwood sidey O.

You have seven more to ring a bell,
Yes, dear mother, we can tell,
And seven more you'll spend in hell,
    Down by the greenwood sidey O.

Sung by Mrs. Theresa Corbett at Conception Harbour, 24th October 1929

B

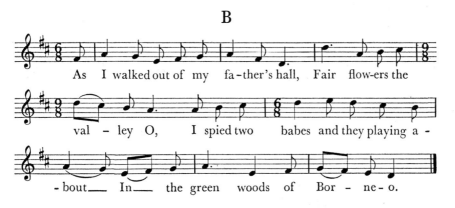

As I walked out of my father's hall,
    Fair flowers the valley O,
I spied two babes and they playing about
    In the green woods of Borneo.

Dear little babes, if you were mine,
I'd dress you up in silk so fine.

Dear mamma, when we were yours,
You neither dressed us in fine nor coarse.

You took a penknife long and sharp,
And you pierced it through our tender hearts.

You took a shawl off your head,
And you spread it over the place we bled.

Dear little babes, O can't you tell
If my poor soul is for heaven or hell.

Heaven is high and hell is low,
And when you die to hell you'll go.

Seven long years ringing a bell,
And for ever burning in eternity.

Sung by Mrs. K. M. Coombs at Portugal Cove, Trepassey Bay, 4th August
1930

C

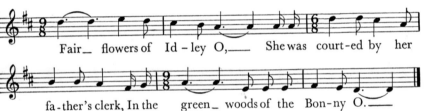

There was a wo - man lived in New York,
Fair_ flowers of Id - ley O,__ She was court-ed by her
fa - ther's clerk, In the green_ woods of the Bon-ny O.__

There was a woman lived in New York,
    Fair flowers of Idley O,
She was courted by her father's clerk,
    In the green woods of the Bonny O.

She had two fair pretty babes of her own,
She prayed to God they'd never be known.

She had no clothes to cover them in,
Only her apron and it was thin.

She had a knife both long and sharp,
She pierced it in the two babes' heart.

She dug a grave both long and deep,
And she put those two pretty babes to sleep.

THE CRUEL MOTHER

She was going to Club [*sic*] one day,
And she thought she saw her babes at play.

O my two pretty babes, I wish you were mine,
I'd dress you up in silk so fine.

O dear mother, when we were yours,
You wouldn't dress us in the richest stores.

O dear mother, it's we can tell
That when you die you'll go to hell.

Sung by Mrs. Violet (John) McCabe at North River, Conception Bay, 15th
October 1929

D

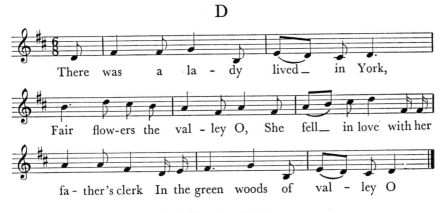

There was a la - dy lived _ in York,
Fair flow-ers the val - ley O, She fell _ in love with her
fa - ther's clerk In the green woods of val - ley O

There was a lady lived in York,
    Fair flowers the valley O,
She fell in love with her father's clerk
    In the green woods of valley O.

She laid her back against the thorns,
And there she had two pretty babes born.

She put them in a cradle deep,
'Twas there she bound them hands and feet.

She took her penknife long and short,
'Twas there she pierced their tender hearts.

As she was walking her father's hall,
Two pretty babes came passing by.

35

Two pretty babes, if you were mine,
I'd dress you in the silk so fine.

O yes, false murderer, when we were yours,
You neither dressed us in coarser clothes.

Two pretty babes, O can you tell
Whether I'll go to heaven or hell.

Yes, false murderer, we can tell
Whether you'll go to heaven or hell.

Heaven is high and hell is low,
   Fair flowers the valley O,
But when you dies to hell you must go
   For murdering those babes of Bonny O.

Sung by Mrs. Jacob Courage at Frenchman's Cove, Garnish, Fortune Bay,
15th July 1930

E

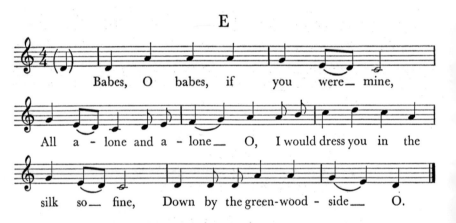

Babes, O babes, if you were mine, All a - lone and a - lone O, I would dress you in the silk so fine, Down by the green-wood - side O.

Sung by Mr. Thomas Sims at Hermitage, 21st July 1930

THE CRUEL MOTHER

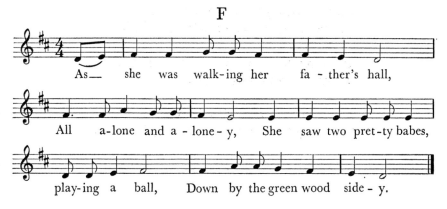

F

As— she was walk-ing her fa - ther's hall,
All a-lone and a - lone - y, She saw two pret-ty babes,
play-ing a ball, Down by the green wood side - y.

Sung by Mrs. Elizabeth (James) Snow at North River, Conception Bay,
15th October 1929

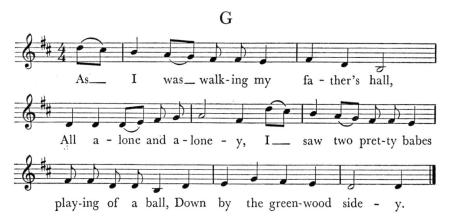

G

As— I was— walk-ing my fa - ther's hall,
All a - lone and a - lone - y, I— saw two pret-ty babes
play-ing of a ball, Down by the green-wood side - y.

As I was walking my father's hall,
    All alone and aloney,
I saw two pretty babes a-playing of a ball,
    Down by the greenwood sidey.

O babes, O babes, if you were mine,
I would dress you up in silk so fine.

Mother, O mother, when we were yours,
You neither dressed us coarse nor fine.

Pretty babes, pretty babes, can you tell
That my poor soul is to be born in hell?

Mother, O mother, it's we can tell
That your poor soul is to be born in hell.

CHILD BALLADS

There's seven years to be born in hell,
And seven more to be ringing of a bell.

And seven more to be a stone in the street
Under men and horses' feet.

And after that you will take a flight
And away to heaven with the angels bright.

Sung by Mr. William Snow (73) at Harbour Grace, 12th October 1929

6 CAPTAIN WEDDERBURN'S COURTSHIP

A

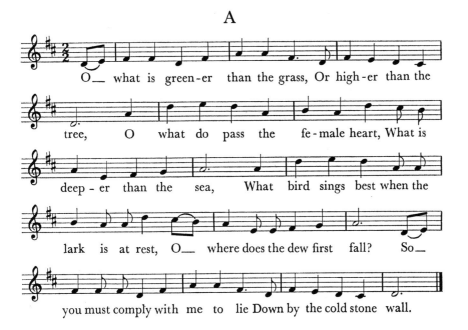

O— what is green-er than the grass, Or high-er than the tree, O what do pass the fe-male heart, What is deep-er than the sea, What bird sings best when the lark is at rest, O— where does the dew first fall? So— you must comply with me to lie Down by the cold stone wall.

O what is greener than the grass,
Or higher than the tree,
O what do pass the female heart,
What is deeper than the sea,
What bird sings best when the lark is at rest,
O where does the dew first fall?
So you must comply with me to lie
Down by the cold stone wall.

O death is greener than the grass,
The sun is higher than the tree,
The devil he passes the female's heart,
Hell is deeper than the sea,
The thrush sings best when the lark is at rest,
On the grass the dew first falls,
So I'll not comply with you to lie
Down by the cold stone wall.

But you must for my breakfast get
A fish without a bone,
And for my dinner you must get
A cherry without a stone,

And for my supper you must get
A bird without a gall,
Or you must comply with me to lie
Down by the cold stone wall.

O when the fish is in its sporn
You know it has no bone,
And when the cherry is in full bloom
You know it has no stone,
The dove she is a gentle bird,
She flies without a gall,
So I'll not comply with you to lie
Down by the cold stone wall.

Sung by Mrs. Mary McCabe at North River, Conception Bay, 17th October
1929

B

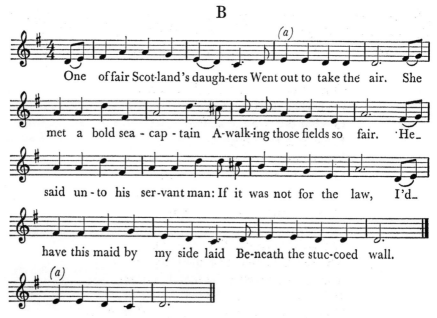

One of fair Scotland's daughters Went out to take the air. She
met a bold sea-cap-tain A-walk-ing those fields so fair. 'He
said un-to his ser-vant man: If it was not for the law, I'd
have this maid by my side laid Be-neath the stuc-coed wall.

One of fair Scotland's daughters
Went out to take the air.
She met a bold sea-captain
A-walking those fields so fair.
He said unto his servant man:
If it was not for the law,
I'd have this maid by my side laid
Beneath the stuccoed wall.

CAPTAIN WEDDERBURN'S COURTSHIP

You must get me for my breakfast
A fish without a bone,
And for my dinner you must get
A cherry without a stone,
And for my supper you must get
A bird without a gall,
Before I'll comply with you to lie
Beneath the stuccoed wall.

When a fish it is for sporned
In it there is no bone,
And when a cherry's in blossom
In it there is no stone,
The dove she is a gentle bird,
She flies without a gall,
So you must comply with me to lie
Beneath the stuccoed wall.

You must get for me some of the fruit
That in November grows,
You must get for me a new slip
Bound with never thread worn through it,
A sparrow's horn and a priest unborn
For to wed us at our call,
Before I'll comply with you to lie
Beneath the stuccoed wall.

My father has some of the fruit
That in November grows,
My mother has a new slip
Bound with never thread worn through it,
A sparrow's horn is easy got,
There's one on every claw,
But the priest unborn I cannot call,
So I'll leave this stuccoed wall.

Sung by Mrs. K. M. Coombs at Portugal Cove, Trepassey Bay, 4th August
1930

7 LORD BATEMAN

OR

LORD AKEMAN

(*Young Beichan*)

A

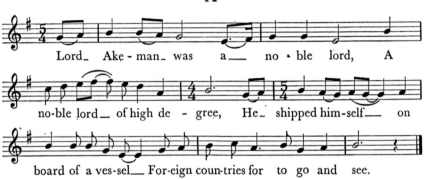

Lord Akeman was a noble lord,
A noble lord of high degree,
He shipped himself on board of a vessel
Foreign countries for to go and see.

He sailèd East and he sailèd West
Until he came to proud Turkey.
'Twas there he was taken and put in prison
Until his life was most weary.

By the side of the prison there grew a tree,
It grew so mighty, stout and long.
He was tied to that right round his middle
Until his life was almost gone.

The gaoler had one only daughter,
One of the fairest creatures I have ever seen.
She stole the keys of her father's prison,
And said Lord Akeman she would set free.

Have you got houses, or have you got land?
Or is any of Northumberland belongs to thee?
What would you give to any fair maiden
Who from this prison would set you free?

42

LORD BATEMAN OR LORD AKEMAN

Yes, I've got houses and I've got land,
And half Northumberland belongs to me.
I would give it all to any lady
Who from this prison would set me free.

Seven long years they made a promise,
And fourteen days he kept [to keep] it strong:
If you don't wed with no other woman,
Sure I won't wed with no other man.

O seven long years have passed and over,
And fourteen days being well known to her,
She packed up her mosky clothing,
And she said Lord Akeman she'd go to see.

And when she sees Lord Akeman's castle
So merrily she rang the bell.
Who's there, who's there? asked the proud young porter,
I pray now unto me tell.

Is Lord Akeman within? she says.
Or is her ladyship within that hall?
O yes, O yes, says the proud young porter,
It's just after bringing a young bride in.

Go tell him to send me a slice of his best bread,
And a bottle of his best wine,
And not to forget the fair young maiden
Who released him from his close confine.

Away, away ran the proud young porter,
Down on his knees he fell to pray,
Saying: I have seen one of the fairest creatures
That ever my eyes would wish to see.

On every finger she has rings,
And on one of them she has got three,
And the golden robes around her middle,
I know Northumberland belongs to she.

Lord Akeman rose then in a passion
And threw his sword in pieces three,

Saying: I'll go no more to foreign countries
Since young Sophia have a-crossed the sea.

Then up speaks the young bride's mother,
Who was never known to speak so free,
Saying: Are you going to leave my daughter
Since young Sophia have a-crossed the sea?

I own my bride I made out of your daughter,
It's neither the better nor the worse for thee.
She came to me in a horse and saddle
And I'll send her home in a coach and three.

Sung by Mr. William Holloway at King's Cove, Bonavista Bay, 25th
September 1929

B

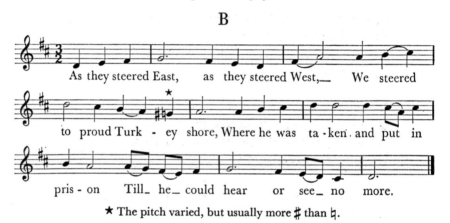

As they steered East,   as they steered West,____   We steered
to proud Turk - ey shore, Where he was ta -ken. and put in
pris - on   Till_ he_ could hear   or see_ no   more.

★ The pitch varied, but usually more ♯ than ♮.

As they steered East, as they steered West,
We steered to proud Turkey shore,
Where he was taken and put in prison
Till he could hear or see no more.

They bored a hole in his left shoulder,
And in the hole they planted a tree.
They had him chained all by the middle
Until his life was quite weary.

The Turkish king had one only daughter,
One only daughter of a high degree,
She stole the keys of her father's treasure,
And said Lord Bateman she would set free.

LORD BATEMAN or LORD AKEMAN

Where she went down in her father's cellar,
Dipped up a jug of the clearest wine,
And every health they drank to each other,
Saying, I wish, Lord Bateman, that you were mine.

Seven years they made a vow,
Seven more on it to stand.
He said he'd wed no other lady
Till Susie [Sophie] Hines had wed a man.

And seven years being nearly ended,
And seven more it's going three,
When she packed up all her rich, gay clothing,
And said Lord Bateman she would go see.

She went down on her father's quay,
She hired a ship, a ship of fame,
As she packed up all her rich gay clothing,
And said Lord Bateman she would go see.

O when she came to Lord Bateman's castle,
Rapped so boldly at the ring.
Who's there, who's there? cries the young proud porter,
Rap so boldly, but can't come in.

Is this Lord Bateman's castle? she cries,
Or is the lord himself within?
O yes, O yes, cries the young proud porter,
This very day brought a young bride in.

Away, away goes the young proud porter,
As fast as lightning away goes he,
Until he came to Lord Bateman's chamber,
Down on his bended knees he fell.

O seven years, my lord, I have served you,
Seven more it's going and three,
The fairest lady stands at your castle
That ever my two eyes have seen.

She has gold rings on every finger,
And on her middle one she has three,

CHILD BALLADS

She got more gold clothing around her middle
Would Lord Bateman and your castle free.

She told you to send one cut of your bread
And a bottle of your wine so strong,
And not to forget that young fair lady
That set you free from your iron bands.

He stamped his feet all on the plancheon,
And he bent the table in splinters three.
I'm going to forsake my wedded wife,
Since Sophie Hines has crossed the sea.

Then up speaks this young bride's mother,
These very words to him did say:
Are you going to forsake your wedded wife,
Since Sophie Hines has crossed the sea?

Your daughter she is but tall and handsome,
She is well featured in every degree,
She came to me in a horse and saddle,
She will go home in a coach and three.

Sung by Miss Joanna Murphy at Kit Hughes, Conception Harbour, 22nd
October 1929

C

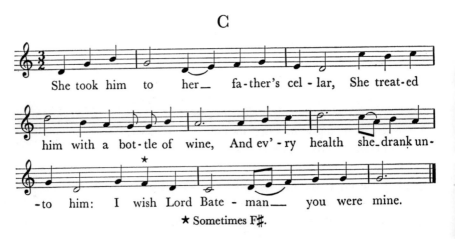

She took him to her father's cellar, She treated him with a bottle of wine, And ev'ry health she drank unto him: I wish Lord Bateman you were mine.

★ Sometimes F♯.

Sung by Mrs. Charles Piercey at St. Jacques, Fortune Bay, 17th July 1930

46

8 FAIR MARGARET AND SWEET WILLIAM

A

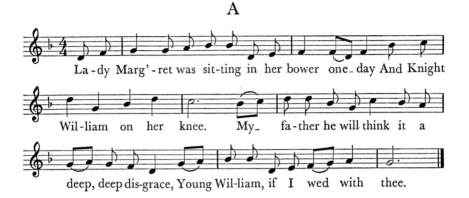

La-dy Marg'-ret was sit-ting in her bower one day And Knight Wil-liam on her knee. My fa-ther he will think it a deep, deep dis-grace, Young Wil-liam, if I wed with thee.

Lady Margaret was sitting in her bower one day
And Knight William on her knee.
My father he will think it a deep, deep disgrace,
Young William, if I wed with thee.

You'd better mind what you're saying, Lady Margaret, he said,
You'd better mind what you're saying to me,
For before three days they are to an end,
A rakish wedding you may see.

Lady Margaret was sitting in her bower next day,
Combing her yellow hair,
And who should she spy there a-riding up close by,
Was Knight William and his lady fair.

She threw away her ivory tooth-comb,
She tossed back her yellow hair,
And out of her bower this fair lady ran
And she was never more seen there.

Young William he woke in the middle of the night,
And unto his lady did say:
Saying: I must go to see Lady Margaret, says he,
By the lief of you, lady.

For I dreamed a dream, a terrible dream,
I'm afraid it's not for our good.
I dreamed that my love was entangled with a swan
And my bride's bed flowing with blood.

47

I dreamed that I saw Lady Margaret, he said,
Standing at my bed-feet,
Saying: The lily and the rose they are covered up with clothes,
And I am in my cold winding-sheet.

He rode till he came to Lady Margaret's bower,
Where so loudly he knocked at the ring,
And none was so ready as her youngest brother there,
He came down in deep mourning.

What mourn you, what mourn you, Knight William? he said,
What mourn you so deeply unto me?
O we are in mourning for our sister dear,
Who died for loving of thee.

O who might eat some of her cake, he did say,
Or who might drink some of her wine,
Or who might ever live till this time tomorrow night,
He will drink some of mine.

Lady Margaret she died in the middle of the night,
And so did Knight William, the Squire.
And out of Lady Margaret there sprung a rose
And out of young William a briar.

And now our love-wars are all at an end,
And all things must be forgot,
For the branch and the briar they both grew up together
And they tied in a true lovers' knot.

Sung by Mrs. Mary McCabe at North River, Conception Bay, 17th October
1929

FAIR MARGARET AND SWEET WILLIAM

B

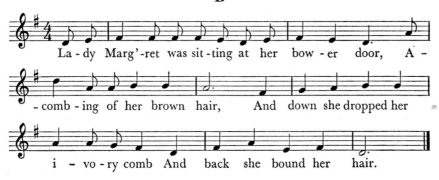

La - dy Marg'-ret was sit-ting at her bow - er door, A -
- comb - ing of her brown hair, And down she dropped her
i - vo - ry comb And back she bound her hair.

Sung by Mrs. Elizabeth Cox at Gaultois, Hermitage Bay, 22nd July 1930

C

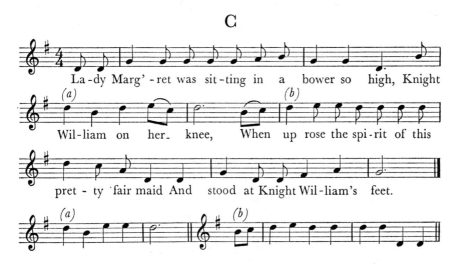

La -dy Marg' - ret was sit -ting in a bower so high, Knight
Wil-liam on her_ knee, When up rose the spi-rit of this
pret - ty 'fair maid And stood at Knight Wil-liam's feet.

Sung by Mrs. Margaret Quilter (74) at Harbour Grace, Conception Bay,
8th October 1929

9 SWEET WILLIAM'S GHOST

A

Lady Marg'ret was sitting in her own loy-al bower, 'Twas built of lime and _ stone,_ La-dy Marg'-ret was sit-ting in her own loy-al bower, When she heard a dead man's moan, When she heard a _ dead man's moan.

Lady Margaret was sitting in her own loyal[1] bower,
'Twas built of lime and stone,
Lady Margaret was sitting in her own loyal bower,
When she heard a dead man's moan.

Now is it my father the king? she cries,
Or is it my brother John?
Or is my own Willie, she said,
From Scotland here have come?

No 'tis not the king, he replied,
It is not your brother John,
But it is your own dear Willie
From Scotland here have come.

Did you bring to me any token of love,
Did you bring to me a ring,
Did you bring to me any token at all
That a true love ought to bring?

[1] Probably 'royal'. The words 'loyal' and 'royal' are sometimes confused by folk singers.

SWEET WILLIAM'S GHOST

No, I've brought to you no token at all,
I've brought to you no ring,
But I've brought to you my winding-sheet
That my body lies mouldering in.

Now in crossing over the frozen plain
On a cold and a stormy night,
In crossing the plains of a cold winter's night
In a dead man's company.

Now when they came to the old churchyard,
Where the graves were mossy green,
Saying: Here is my place of residence
For me to take a sleep.

Is there any room at your head? she said,
Or any at your feet,
Or any room about you
For me to take a sleep?

No, my father is at my head, he said,
My mother is at my feet,
And there's three little devils
For my soul to take.

One of them is for my drunkenness,
And the other is for my pride,
And the other is for deluding of fair pretty maids
And staying out late in the night.

Sung by Michael Caroll, Senior, at Placentia, 5th July 1930

B

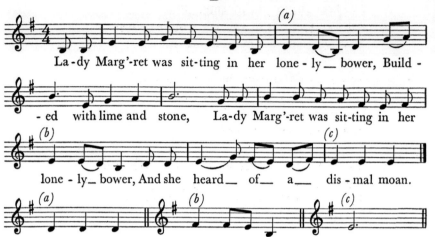

Lady Margaret was sitting in her lonely bower,
Builded with lime and stone,
Lady Margaret was sitting in her lonely bower,
And she heard of a dismal moan.

Is this my father the king? she cries,
Or is it my brother John?
Or is it my true love, Knight William? she cries,
From Scotland he has come.

It's not your father the king, he cries,
Nor yet your brother John.
But it is your true love, Knight William, he cries,
From Scotland he has come.

Do you bring to me any apparel, she said,
Or do you bring to me a ring,
Or do you bring to me any token at all
That a true love ought to bring?

I brought to you no apparel, he said,
I've brought to you no ring,
All I brought to you is my cold winding-sheet
That my poor body lies in.

There's one requestion I'll ask of thee,
I hope you will grant to me,

SWEET WILLIAM'S GHOST

That is my faith and a troth, he said,
Lady Margaret, I'll leave in pledge with thee.
  (I leaved in pledge with thee.)

Your faith and a troth, I'll not bring to you,
Or any such a thing,
Until you'll take me to yonder church
And wed me with a ring.

O God forbid, Lady Margaret, he said,
That ever that should be
  (That any such thing should be)
That the dead should arise and marry the quick
And vanish away from thee.

She took her petticoats in her hands
And they above her knees,
And it's over the hills of a cold winter's night
In a dead man's company,

Until they came to the mossy green bank
Where the graves been grassy green.
  (They walked over hills and grassy plains
  Till they came to a grassy grave.)
There's my home, Lady Margaret, he said,
And the place I do dwell in.
  (And the place where I'm to rest.)

Have you any room at your bed's head,
Or any at your feet,
Or have you any room at all
That I lay down to sleep?

My father he's at my bed's head,
And my mother is at my feet,
And there's three hell hounds all around me
Waiting my poor soul to keep.

One of them's for my drunkenness,
And the other's for my pride,
And the other is for deluding a fair pretty maid
And staying out late by night.

CHILD BALLADS

She took her hand all from her side
And struck him all on the breast.
Here is my faith and a troth, Knight William,
God grant your soul to rest.

I thank you, Lady Margaret, he said,
I thank thee kinderly,
If ever the dead is allowed to pray for the quick,
I must be allowed to pray for thee.
   (If the living is allowed to pray for the dead,
    I hope you'll pray for me.)
The words in brackets are as sung by Mr. John McCabe, Mrs. Boone's son.

Sung by Mrs. Emma Boone at North River, Conception Bay, 15th October
1929

C

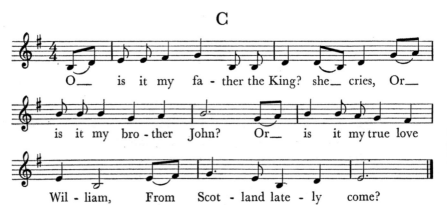

Sung by Mr. John McCabe at North River, Conception Bay, 15th October
1929

D

Sung by Miss Zeala McCabe at Harbour Grace, 8th October 1929

SWEET WILLIAM'S GHOST

E

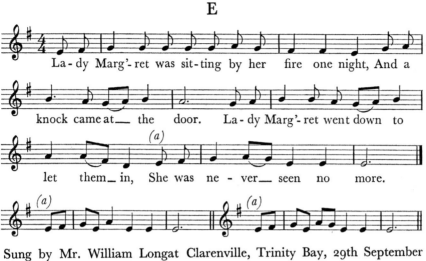

La-dy Marg'-ret was sit-ting by her fire one night, And a knock came at___ the door. La-dy Marg'-ret went down to let them___ in, She was ne - ver___ seen no more.

Sung by Mr. William Longat Clarenville, Trinity Bay, 29th September 1929

F

Sung by Mr. Thomas Sims at Hermitage, 21st July 1930

G

O is it my fa - ther the King? she — cried, Or —
is it my bro - ther — John? Or — is it my true love
Wil - li -am? she cried, From — Scot - land — he — has come.

Sung by Mrs. Michael Cheeseman and Gordon Cheeseman (her son, aged 19) at Marystown, Placentia Bay, 12th July 1930

H

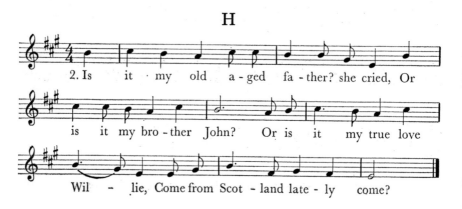

2. Is it · my old a - ged fa - ther? she cried, Or
is it my bro - ther John? Or is it my true love
Wil - lie, Come from Scot - land late - ly come?

Sung by Mrs. Patrick and Mrs. Mathew Brennan at Stock Cove, Bonavista Bay, 9th September 1929

SWEET WILLIAM'S GHOST

I

Is there a - ny room at your head? she_ cried, Or a - ny down by your feet? Or a - ny_ room at your right hand side That I can lie_ and_ sleep?

Sung by Mrs. Anne Aylward at Stock Cove, Bonavista Bay, 14th September 1929

10 THE UNQUIET GRAVE

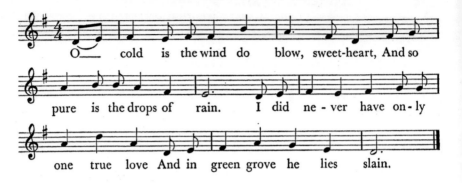

O— cold is the wind do blow, sweet-heart, And so
pure is the drops of rain. I did ne - ver have on - ly
one true love And in green grove he lies slain.

O cold is the wind do blow, sweetheart,
And so pure is the drops of rain.
I did never have only one true love
And in green grove he lies slain.

Sure I'll do as much for my true love
As any one that may,
I'll sit, I'll mourn all on his grave
For a twelve month and a day.

The twelve month and one day expired
And the ghost began to speak:
O what is this is on my grave
And will not let me sleep?

O once I was your own true love,
I do sit on your grave.
One kiss all from your cold clay lips,
That is all I do a-crave.

O if you're to kiss my cold clay lips,
Your life won't last you long;
And if you're to kiss my cold clay lips,
My breath smells heavy strong.

'Tis down in garden green, sweetheart,
Where you and I had walked,
The nicest flower that ever I saw
Was withered from the stalk.

THE UNQUIET GRAVE

The stalk has withered dry, sweetheart,
And will not grow no more,
We'll hoist our sails before the main
And our ship must bore away.[1]

Sung by Mrs. Maggie Day at Fortune Harbour, 1st October 1929

11 MATTHY GROVES
(*Little Musgrave*)

A

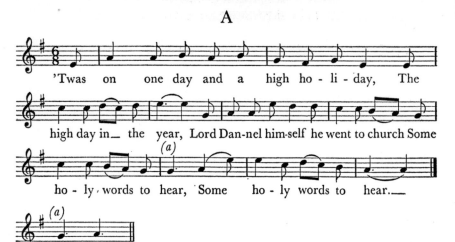

'Twas on one day and a high holiday,
The high day in the year,
Lord Dannel himself he went to church
Some holy words to hear,
Some holy words to hear.

What news, what news, my little post boy,
What news thou broughtest me?
Bad news, bad news and very bad news,
The worst of news to thee.

Is any of my buildings down,
Or any of my bowers gone,
Or is my wife now in the bed
With a daughter or a son?

There is none of your buildings down,
Nor none of your bowers gone,
This very night young Marshall Groves
Is in bed with your gay lady.

If this is the truth that art telling to me,
It will be the better for thee;
If this a lie that art telling to me,
I'll hang thee on a tree.

MATTHY GROVES

I would not and I dare not,
I would not for my life;
The rings she had on her fair finger,
I know 'twas Lord Dannel's wife.

Lord Dannel callèd all his men,
He ordered them all in his room;
He ordered not a word to be spoke,
Nor yet the horn to blow.

But one of his men went against his will,
He holloed both loud and shrill:
A man that's in bed with another man's wife,
'Tis time to be jogging away.

I thought I heard Lord Dannel's voice,
I thought I heard him say:
A man that's in bed with another man's wife,
'Tis time to be jogging away.

Huddle me up and cuddle me in,
And shelter me from the cold;
It's only the old blind shepherd
Just driving his sheep to fold.

He huddled her up and he cuddled her in,
They both fell off to sleep.
Early next morning when they awoke,
Lord Dannel stood at the bedside.

How do you like my bed, he said,
And how do you like my sheet,
And how do you like my gay lady
That lies in your arms asleep?

It's well I like your bed, he said,
And better I like your sheet,
But the best of all is the gay lady
That lies in my arms asleep.

Arise, arise, young Marshall Groves,
Some raiment to put on;

I'd never have it to say in my life
That I killèd a naked man.

I have two swords all by my side,
Which cost me right of my purse,
And you may take the best of them
And I will take the worst.

And you may strike the very first blow,
And I will strike the other;
I cannot say any fairer than that
If it was my true born brother.

The very first blow Marshall gave,
He wounded Lord Dannel full sore;
The very first Lord Dannel gave,
Marshall Groves can't rise no more.

He took his gay lady on his knee,
Saying: Between Marshall Groves and she,
I'd rather have Marshall Groves' little finger
Than all thy whole body.

Then the little birds they sang for joy,
The bells did toll for sorrow;
Lord Dannel he killèd his wife today,
And he's going to be hung tomorrow.

Sung by Mr. George Taylor at Grole, Hermitage Bay, 23rd July 1930

MATTHY GROVES

B

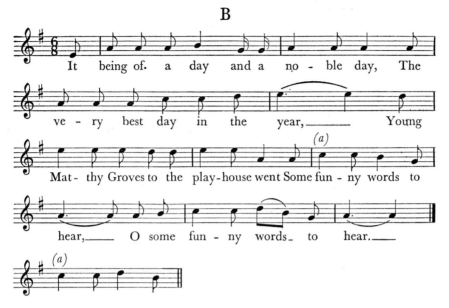

It being of a day and a noble day,
The very best day in the year,
Young Matthy Groves to the play-house went
Some funny words to hear,
O some funny words to hear.

Some were dressed in robes of satin
And more were dressed in silk,
And who should come in but Lord Allen's wife
And her skin as white as milk.

She lookèd up and she lookèd down,
And who should she spy
But this very night young Matthy Groves
In bed with me must lie.

He said: I would not, nor I cannot,
Nor I would not for my life,
For by the ring that's on your finger
You are Lord Allen's wife.

She said: If I am Lord Allen's wife,
What is that to thee?
For Lord Allen is gone to Newcastle
King Henry for to see.

63

The little foot-page was standing by,
He took to his heels and run,
And when he got to the riverside
He fell to his breast and swum.

He swum till he come to King Henry's door,
And he knocked so loud at the ring,
And nobody so ready as Lord Allen himself
For to let that foot-page in.

Is there any of my castles fallen down,
Or any of my towers won,
Or is my fair lady put to bed
With a daughter or a son?

There's none of your castles fallen down,
Nor none of your towers won,
But this very night young Matthy Groves
In bed with your lady's come.

He called up all his merry men
And placed them in a row,
And he ordered not one word to be spoken
Nor neither a horn to blow.

But one of his merry men
To gain his mistress's will,
He put a horn all to his mouth
And he blowed both loud and shrill.

I think I hear Lord Allen's horn,
And I think I hear him say:
A man is in bed with another man's wife
And it's time to be jogging away.

You do not hear Lord Allen's horn
Nor you do not hear him say:
A man is in bed with another man's wife.
You can sleep till the break of day.

Come huddle me, come cuddle me,
And keep me from the cold,

MATTHY GROVES

For it is like father's shepherd's boy
A-putting his sheep in fold.

He huddled her, he cuddled her,
Till they both fell fast asleep,
And when they woke to her surprise
Lord Allen stood at their feet.

Then how do you like my bed, he said,
And how do you like my sheet,
And how do you like my fair lady
Lies in your arms to sleep?

Very well I like your bed, he said,
But better I like your sheet,
And better I like your fair lady
Lies in my arms to sleep.

Then rise, O rise, young Matthy Groves,
And some of your clothes put on,
For it'll never be said when I am dead
I killed a naked man.

I would not, nor I cannot,
Nor I would not for my life,
For you got two swords by your side
And I got ne'er a knife.

If I got two swords by my side
I paid for them in my purse,
Then you can take the best of them
And I will take the worst.

You can take the very first blow,
And I will take the other;
And what fairer could Lord Allen say,
If you do not he would burn both.

The very first stroke young Matthy he made,
He wounded Lord Allen sore;
The very next stroke Lord Allen made,
Young Groves he was no more.

Then he called up his fair lady,
And daddled her on his knee,
Saying: You choose, you choose, my fair lady,
Between young Groves and me.

Then well I like your lips,
But better I like your chin,
But better I like you in the bed
Than all your chief or king.

The bells did ring, the birds did sing,
. . . .
Lord Allen killed his wife today
And he will be hanged tomorrow.

Sung by Mr. William Snow at Harbour Grace, 12th October 1929

12 GEORGE COLLINS

As I rov-ed out one morn-ing in May, The mea-dows they were in full bloom,— A-watch-ing the stone a pret-ty fair girl, A watch-ing the mar-ble stone.—

As I roved out one morning in May,
The meadows they were in full bloom,
A-watching the stone a pretty fair girl,
A-watching the marble stone.

She holloaed, she bollowed, she screamed with her might
She wrung her slim hands to the stars,
To the stars from heaven was twinkling down,
And she dreamed Young Collins was dead.

Collins he went to his own father's door,
Long hours before it was day.
O rise, O rise, dear father, he cried,
Rise and let me in.

His own true love came to the door.
Whose corpse is this? she cried.
It's the corpse of Young Collins, she said,
An old true love of mine.

Bring in the corpse, she said,
I'll trim it with ribbons so fine;
I'll take the last [kiss] from his clear cold lips
Where ten thousand times he kissed mine.

Bring in the sheet, she said,
Till I fix it with linen so fine.
Today it lies over Young Collins, she said,
And tomorrow it will be over mine.

The news went out in old Dublin's town,
And hung upon Dublin's gate.
There's six pretty maids a-died that night,
'Twas all for Young Collins's sake.

If I shall die this very same night,
I'd die, I hope and I will,
Bring me under the old green tree,
Where Young Collins's body did dwell.

Sung by Mrs. Mary Tibbs at Trinity, 13th September 1929

13 LAMKIN

A

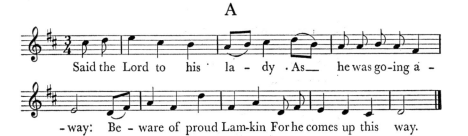

Said the Lord to his la - dy . As— he was go-ing a - way: Be - ware of proud Lam-kin For he comes up this way.

Said the lord to his lady
As he was going away:
Beware of proud Lamkin,
For he comes up this way.

What do I care for proud Lamkin,
Or any of his men,
When my doors are well bolted
And my windows shut in.

He was scarce gone one hour,
When proud Lamkin came by;
He knocked at the hall door
And the nurse let him in.

O where is your master?
Is he not without?
He's gone to old England,
Cried the false nurse.

O where is your mistress?
Is she not within?
She's up in her bed-chamber
With the windows barred in.

How am I to get at her?
Proud Lamkin did cry.
O here is young Sir Johnson,
Pierce him and he'll cry.

He took out his bodkin,
And pierced young Sir Johnson,

And made the blood trinkle
Right down his toes.

O mistress, dearest mistress,
How can you sleep so fast?
Can't you hear your young Sir Johnson
A-crying his last.

I can't pacify him
On the nurse-milk or pap;
I pray you come down,
Quieten him on your lap.

How can I come downstairs
On such a cold winter's night,
No spark of fire burning,
No candle alight?

You've got two white holland sheets
As white as snow;
I pray you come down
By the light of them so.

As she was coming downstairs
Not thinking much harm,
Proud Lamkin awaited,
Took her by the arm.

I have got you, I have got you,
Proud Lamkin did cry,
For years I have waited,
But I have got you at last.

O spare me my life, she cries,
For one, two o'clock,
And I'll give you all the money
That you will carry on your back.

If you'll give me the money
Like the sand on the shore,
I'll not keep my bright sword
From your white skin so free.

LAMKIN

O spare me my life, she cries,
For one half an hour,
I'll give to you my nurse,
Although she's my flower.

O where is your nurse?
Go send her to me;
She can hold the silver basin
While your heart's blood runs free.

False nurse was my friend, she cries,
But now she's my foe;
She can hold the silver basin
While my heart's blood do flow.

There was blood in the nursery
And blood in the hall
And blood on the stairs
And her heart's blood was all.

Proud Lamkin was taken
To the gallows to die,
And false nurse she was burned
In a fire near by.

Sung by Mrs. Violet McCabe at North River, Conception Bay, 19th October
1929

B

1. Said Lord Doug-las to his la - dy In__ walk-ing one
day: Be - ware of Lord Lam-kin When he comes this way.
2. Why need I be - ware of Lord Lam-kin, she says, With my
doors__ well__ bolt - ed And my win-dows barred in?

Sung by Mrs. Theresa Corbett at Conception Harbour, 23rd October 1929

CHILD BALLADS

C

The lord to the la-dy Was walk-ing the quay, Said the
lord to the la-dy: Are you 'fraid of Lam-kin?

Sung by Mrs. May Joseph at Marystown, Placentia Bay, 10th July 1930

D

Proud Lam-kin was ta-ken and con-demned for to
die, And the false heart-ed maid-én was burned a-long-side.

Sung by Mr. Joseph Quann at Rencontre, Fortune Bay, 18th July 1930

14 WILLIE o' WINSBURY

A

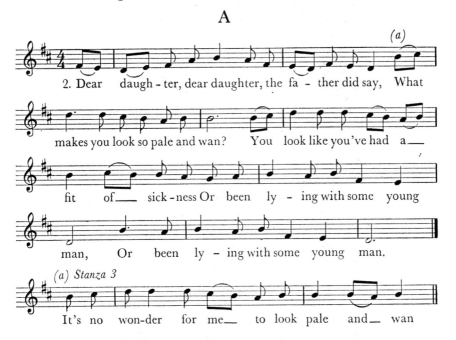

2. Dear daugh-ter, dear daughter, the fa-ther did say, What makes you look so pale and wan? You look like you've had a— fit of— sick-ness Or been ly-ing with some young man, Or been ly-ing with some young man.

(a) Stanza 3

It's no won-der for me— to look pale and— wan

As she was looking over her father's castle wall
When she saw a ship sailing in.

Dear daughter, dear daughter, the father did say,
What makes you look so pale and wan?
You look like you've had a fit of sickness
Or been lying with some young man. [*bis*]

Dear father, dear father, the daughter did say,
It's no wonder for me to look pale and wan,
For all the troubles of my poor heart,
My true love is long at sea.

Is he any lord, duke or noble man,
Or a man of high degree,
Or is he one of our seven sea-boys
That ploughs o'er the raging sea?

He is no lord, duke or noble man,
Nor a man of high degree,
But he is one of our seven sea-boys
That ploughs o'er the raging sea.

73

Dear daughter, dear daughter, the father did say,
It's truth you're telling unto me,
For tomorrow morning at eight o'clock
It is hangèd he will surely be.

Dear father, dear father, the daughter did say,
It's truth you're telling unto me,
For if you hang my own true love
You won't get no good of me.

Her father called down his seven sea-boys,
By one, by two, by three,
And Sweet Willie that always used to be the first
But the last came down was he.

He came down, he came tripping down,
He was clothèd all in silk,
His cheeks was of the roses red,
His skin was as white as the milk.

Dear daughter, dear daughter, the father did say,
It's no wonder that thanks must be,
For if I was a woman instead of a man
I would die for the love of he.

Will you marry my daughter, he says,
And take her by the hand?
And you can come and live with me
And be heir over all my land.

I will marry your daughter, he says,
And take her by the hand,
But I won't come to live with you
Nor a fig for none of your land.

If you can give her one guinea,
I can give her thirty-three,
Although you calls me the young Barber
That ploughs o'er the raging sea.

Sung by Mrs. Janie Augot at Rencontre, Fortune Bay, 18th July 1930

WILLIE o' WINSBURY

B

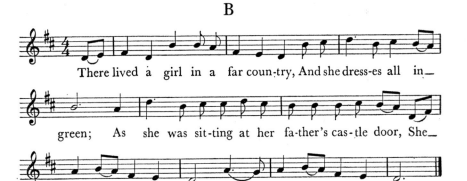

There lived a girl in a far coun-try, And she dress-es all in_ green; As she was sit-ting at her fa-ther's cas-tle door, She_ saw a_ ship sail in, She_ saw a_ ship sail in.

There lived a girl in a far country,
And she dresses all in green;
As she was sitting at her father's castle door,
She saw a ship sail in. [*bis*]

O daughter, O daughter, the father cries,
Why do you look so pale?
Have you had some heavy sickness,
Or are you in love with some young man?

O father, O father, the daughter cries,
Why I am looking pale,
I have had no heavy sickness,
But I'm in love with some young man.

Is it a duke or a wealthy squire,
Or a man of a high degree,
Or is it one of my seven sailors bold
That ploughs the raging sea?

He's not a duke, nor a squire, she says,
Nor a man of a high degree,
But he is one of your seven sailors bold
That ploughs the raging sea.

O daughter, O daughter, the father cries,
If it's true what you're telling me,
Tomorrow morning at eight o'clock
It's hung your love shall be.

O father, O father, the daughter cries,
If it's true what you're telling me,
If my love is to be hung tomorrow morning
You'll get no good of me.

The king called down his seven sailors bold,
By one, by two, by three,
Where Willie was always the first on deck,
The last came down was he.

Young Willie came down step by step,
All dressed in a suit of silk,
With his two rosy cheeks and his curly bright hair
And his skin as white as milk.

O daughter, O daughter, the father cries,
I'll lay no blame to thee,
For if I was a woman instead of a man,
I'd die today for he.

Will you marry my daughter, he said,
And take her by the hand?
Then will you come and dine with me
And be head over all my land?

Yes, I will marry your daughter, he says,
And I'll take her by the hand,
Then I will go and dine with you,
But I don't want your land.

For where you can give her one guinea,
Why I can give her three,
Although I was one of your seven sailors bold
That ploughed o'er the raging sea.

Sung by Miss Florrie Snow at North River, Conception Bay, 18th October
1929

WILLIE o' WINSBURY

C

There was a la-dy in the north coun-try, She dress-es all in green; As she was sit-ting in her fa-ther's cas-tle door, When she saw a—ship sail-ing in, When she saw a—ship sail-ing in.

Sung by Mrs. Bridget Hall at North River, Conception Bay, 16th October 1929

D

It was of a young la-dy who lived in the East And she dressed her-self all—in green; As—she gazed o-ver her fa-ther's cas-tle wall To see the ships sail-ing, To— see— the ships sail-ing.

Sung by Mrs. May (James) McCabe at North River, Conception Bay, 15th October 1929

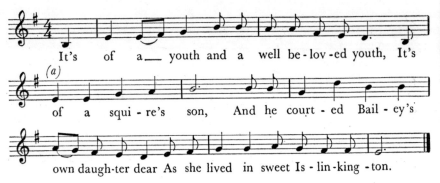

It's of a — youth and a well be-lov-ed youth, It's
of a squi-re's son, And he court-ed Bail-ey's
own daugh-ter dear As she lived in sweet Is-lin-king-ton.

It's of a youth and a well belovèd youth,
It's of a squire's son,
And he courted Bailey's own daughter dear,
As she lived in sweet Islinkington.[1]

As she was going up the street
And he came riding down,
Where she took his horse all by the bridle side
And she swung herself right round.

O where are you going, my fair pretty maid?
O where are you going? cried she.
I am in search of the Bailey's daughter dear
As she lived in sweet Islinkington.

The Bailey's daughter of Islinkington,
She's dead and don't you know,
The Bailey's daughter of Islinkington,
She's been dead, sir, this long time ago.

If Bailey's daughter is now dead,
I'll sell my milkwhite steed,
And I'll go to some foreign country
Where no one shall never, never know.

The Bailey's daughter is not dead,
She still remains alive,

[1] Islington or Islingtown.

78

THE BAILIFF'S DAUGHTER OF ISLINGTON

And here she is all by the bridle side,
All ready to make you her bride.

How glad was he when he heard of this,
How glad was he to stand,
And how well he knew it was Bailey's daughter dear
With the private mark she had on her hand.

Sung by Mrs. Alice Sims at Pass Island, 24th July 1930

16 THE BAFFLED KNIGHT

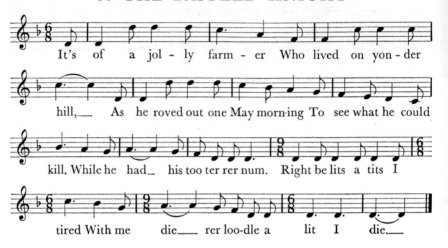

It's of a jol - ly farm - er Who lived on yon - der hill,___ As he roved out one May morn-ing To see what he could kill. While he had_ his too ter rer num. Right be lits a tits I tired With me die___ rer loo-dle a lit I die.___

Sung by Mrs. Violet McCabe at North River, Conception Bay, 17th October 1929

17 THE GYPSY LADDIE

A

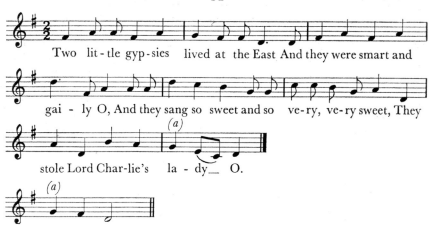

Two lit-tle gyp-sies lived at the East And they were smart and
gai - ly O, And they sang so sweet and so ve-ry, ve-ry sweet, They
stole Lord Char-lie's la - dy— O.

Two little gypsies lived at the East
And they were smart and gaily O,
And they sang so sweet and so very, very sweet,
They stole Lord Charlie's lady O.

So Lord Charlie he came home
Enquiring for his lady O.
Up speaks one of his old servant men,
Saying: She's follow on a gypsy laddie O.

Saying: Will you come home, my fair lady,
Will you come home, my honey,
And will you forsake your own native land
And follow on a gypsy laddie O?

I'll forsake my own native land,
Likewise my lord and Charlie O,
And I'll forsake my own native land
And follow on a gypsy laddie O.

Sung by Mrs. Margaret Quilter at Harbour Grace, 8th October 1929

B

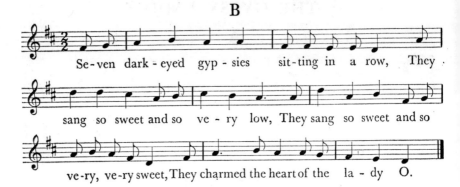

Se-ven dark-eyed gyp-sies sit-ting in a row, They sang so sweet and so ve-ry low, They sang so sweet and so ve-ry, ve-ry sweet, They charmed the heart of the la-dy O.

Seven dark-eyed gypsies sitting in a row,
They sang so sweet and so very low,
They sang so sweet and so very, very sweet,
They charmed the heart of the lady O.

The lady was sitting in her window so high,
Enjoying of her children three;
Some jealousy thought came into her mind,
She would follow the dark-eyed gypsy O.

The old farmer came home in the middle of the night,
Enquiring for his lady O.
I'm afraid, I'm afraid, cried the gay gaging [*sic*] girl,
That she followed the dark-eyed gypsy O.

Hurry up, hurry up and get my team,
With a sword and pistol by my side,
With a sword and pistol by my side,
I will follow the dark-eyed gypsy O.

He rode East and he rode West,
Till he came up to an old farmer,
Saying: Farmer, tell me, tell me true,
Have you seen the dark-eyed gypsy O?

Ride on, ride on, the old farmer cried,
Till you come to yonder valley O,
The prettiest girl that ever I did see
In the arms of the dark-eyed gypsy O.

Last night you were lying on a soft down bed
With a sheet so white as the linen O,

THE GYPSY LADDIE

Tonight you are lying on the hard cold ground
In the arms of the dark-eyed gypsy O.

Sung by Mrs. Wilson Northcott at Gaultois, Hermitage Bay, 22nd July 1930

C

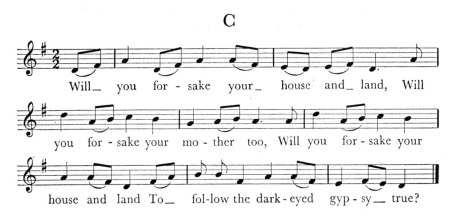

Will— you for - sake your— house and— land, Will
you for - sake your mo - ther too, Will you for - sake your
house and land To— fol-low the dark - eyed gyp - sy— true?

Sung by Mr. Jacob Courage at Frenchman's Cove, Garnish, Fortune Bay,
15th July 1930

D

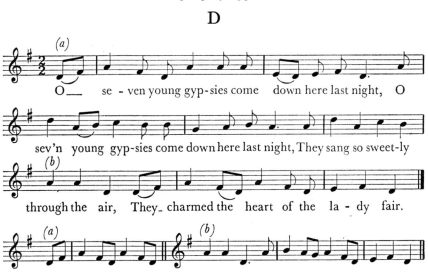

O— se - ven young gyp-sies come down here last night, O
sev'n young gyp-sies come down here last night, They sang so sweet-ly
through the air, They— charmed the heart of the la - dy fair.

Sung by Mrs. May Joseph Mitchell at Marystown, Placentia Bay, 10th July
1930

E

Seven gypsies stood in a row,
They sang so sweetly through the air,

83

They sang, they sang so very, very sweet,
That they charmed the heart of a lady fair.

This fair lady sitting in her castle high,
Smiling on those gypsies.
A noise, a very silly noise ran through her mind
To follow the dark-eyed gypsies true.

That night when her husband he came home
Enquiring for his lady fair.
I'm afraid, I'm afraid, says the old kitchen-maid,
That she followed the dark-eyed gypsies true.

O come saddle my horse, come saddle my team,
And brace my pistols by my side
That I will go chase of the dark-eyed gypsy true.

First they rode West and then they rode North
Till they came to a farmer's door.
O farmer, O farmer, tell me the truth,
Did you see the dark-eyed gypsy true?

Go down, go down in yonder green field [*bis*]
And there you'll find your own true love
In the arms of a dark-eyed gypsy true.

O last night you lay on your feather bed
With blankets round you white as snow,
And tonight you'll lay on the damp cold ground
In the arms of a dark-eyed gypsy true.

O I'll forsake my castle, she said,
O I'll forsake my property,
And my own true love I won't mind
And I'll follow the dark-eyed gypsy true.

I'll eat of the grass and drink of the dew [*3 times*]
And follow the dark-eyed gypsy true.

Sung by Mr. Patrick Hunt at Dunsville, Placentia, 8th July 1930. The tune
was not noted.

18 SIR JAMES THE ROSS
(*Sir James the Rose*)

A

It's all those Scot-tish lords and chiefs Of high war - like name, The

brav - est is — Sir James the Ross, That knight of ma - ny fame.—

It's all those Scottish lords and chiefs
Of high war-like name,
The bravest is Sir James the Ross,
That knight of many fame.

His growth was of the tuft that firmed
That crowned the mountain air,
And waving over his shoulder flew
His locks of yellow hair.

The chief then of the high clan Ross,
That firm undaunted being;
Five hundred warriors drew their swords
Beneath his high command.

In blood to fight twice hard he stood
Against the English king,
And two and twenty opening springs
This blooming youth had seen.

And fair Mathilda dear he loved,
That maid of beauty rare,
Yet Margaret on the Scottish throne
Was never half so fair.

Long had he woo'd and long she refused
With seeming scorn and pride,
Yet oft her eyes confessed the love
Her fearful words denied.

At last she dressed his well-tried feat
And allowed his tender claim,

And vow'd to him her virgin heart
That owned an equal fame.

One night they met as they did walk
Close in a shady wood,
And on the bank beside this brook,
A blooming sulting stood.

Concealed beneath this underwood
A crafty Daniel lay,
A brother to Sir John Graham,
To hear what they would say.

Thus the maid began: Dear sir,
Our passion disapproves
And bids me wed Sir John Graham
And leave the youth I love.

What do I hear is this I vow,
Sir John the Ross replied,
And will Mathilda wed Graham
When sworn to be my bride?

His sword shall sooner pierce my heart
Than rob me of my charm.
He pressed her to his beating breast
Fast locked within his arms.

I spoke to try thy love, she said,
I'll never wed man but thee,
The grave shall be my bridegroom bed
If Graham my husband be.

They parted thus, the sun was set;
Up hasty Daniel flies,
And turn thee, turn thee, beardless youth
He loud insulting cries.

And turned around this fearless chief
And soon his sword he drew,
For Daniel bled before his breast
And pierced his tartans through.

SIR JAMES THE ROSS

It's for my brother's spited love,
His wrong sits on my arm.
Three paces back this youth retired
To save himself from harm.

And turning swift his hand he raised,
Pierced Daniel's head above,
And through the brain and crashing bone
His sharp-edged weapon drove.

He staggered and reeled and tumbled down
Like a lump of breathless clay.
You follow my foe, cries gallant Ross,
And stately drove away.

To the green woods he gave read
Unto Lord Bolden's hall,
And at Mathilda's window stood,
And this began to call:

Is thou asleep, my dear,
Awake, my love, awake.
A luckless lover calls on thee
A long farewell to take.

For I have slain fierce Daniel Graham,
His blood it's on my sword
And far, far distant are my men
That shall desist [assist] their lord.

To Skye I'll now direct my way
Where my two brothers bide;
I'll raise the valiants of that isle
To combat on my side.

Do not go, the maid replies;
With me till morning stay,
For dark and dreary is the night
And dangerous is the way.

All night I'll watch you in the park,
My foot-page back I'll send

In hopes to rouse the Ross's men
Their master to defend.

Beneath the bush she laid him down,
Wrapped within his plaid,
And trembling for her lover's fate
A distance stood the maid.

Swift flew the page over hills and dales
Till in the lonely glen
He met the furious John Graham
And twenty of his men.

Where do you go, little page, he said,
So late who do descend?
I go to rouse the Ross's men
Their master to defend.

For he have slain fair Daniel Graham,
His blood it's on his sword,
And far, far distant are his men
That should assist their lord.

And has he slain my brother dear,
The furious Graham replied,
His honour blast my name, he said,
By me at morning dies.

Tell me where is Sir James the Ross,
I will thee well reward.
He sleeps unto Lord Bolden's park,
Mathilda is his guard.

They picked their staves with furious moves
And scoured along the way;
They reached Lord Bolden's lofty tower
By the dawning of the day.

Mathilda stood outside the gate,
To whom Graham did say:
Have you seen Sir James the Ross last night
Or did he pass this way?

SIR JAMES THE ROSS

Last day at noon, Mathilda cries,
Sir James the Ross passed by;
He picked his staves with furious moves
And onward past did drive.

By this he is at Edinburgh town,
If horse and men him good.
Your page then lied who said he was
Here sleeping in this wood.

She wrung her hands and tore her hair.
Brave Ross thou art betrayed,
And ruined by those very means
For whence I helped thy name.

By this the valiant knight awoke,
The virgin's shriek he heard,
He then rose up and drew his sword
When this fierce band appeared.

Your sword last night my brother slain,
His blood yet dims its shine,
And e'er the setting of the sun
Your blood shall reek on mine.

Your word is well, the chief replied,
But deeds will prove the men.
Set by your men and hand to hand
I'll try what valour can.

O boasting high those cowards heard,
My hearty [haughty?] sword he fear.
In showing from those folding fields
If he'll keep in the rear.

With dauntless steps he onward drove,
And dared him to the fight.
Graham gave back and from his aim
For well he knew its might.

Up comes his foe, his bravest foe,
And sank down beneath his sword,

CHILD BALLADS

And still they scorn the poor revenge
And sought this hearty [haughty?] lord.

Behind him basely came Graham,
And pierced him through the side.
Out spouting comes the crimson tide
And all his tartans dyed.

But still the sword cut not the grip
Nor felled him to the ground,
Till through his enemy's heart with steel
He had forced this mortal wound.

Graham like a tree overthrown with wind
Fell breathless on the clay
And down beside him sinks brave Ross,
A-fainting, dying lay.

The sad Mathilda saw him fall.
O spare his life, she cries,
Lord Bolden's daughter begs his life
Let her not be denied.

Her well-known voice the hero knew,
He raised his half-closed eyes,
And fixes them on the weeping maid
And weakly this replied:

In vain Mathilda begs the life,
My debt shall rest tonight.
My race is run, here doom, my love,
Then closed his eyes and died.

The sword yet warm from his left side
With frantic hand she drew,
I come, Sir James the Ross, she cries,
I come to follow you.

She lain the hilt against the ground,
And bared her snow-white breast,
And fell upon her lover's face
To sink to endless rest.

Sung by Mr. Pat Kiley at Gaskiers, St. Mary's, 29th July 1930

SIR JAMES THE ROSS

B

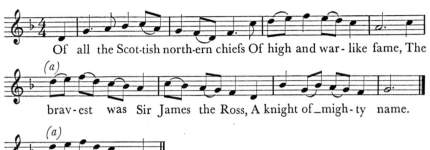

Of all the Scot-tish north-ern chiefs Of high and war-like fame, The

brav-est was Sir James the Ross, A knight of _migh-ty name.

Of all the Scottish northern chiefs
Of high and war-like fame,
The bravest was Sir James the Ross,
A knight of mighty name.

The fair Mathilda dear he loved,
A maid of high renown

. . . .
And bid her wed Sir James the Ross.

. . . .
. . . .

Art thou asleep, Mathilda dear?
Awake, my love, I say,
A luckless lover on thee calls
A long farewell to take.

For I have slain Sir Donald Graham,
His blood lies on my sword,
And far, far distant are my men,
They can't assist their lord.

To Skye I'll now direct my way
Where my two brothers abide,
And rouse the combat of the . . .
And combat on my side.

O do not go, the maid replied,
With me till morning stay,

91

For dark and distant is the road
And dangerous is the way.

All night I'll watch you in the park,
My faithful page I'll send
To run and raise the Ross's clan
Their master to defend.

Swift ran the page o'er hill and dale
Till in a lonely glen
He met the fierce Sir John Graham
With fifth of his men.

Where goest thou, little page, he said,
So late who did thee send?
I have to raise the Ross's clan
Their master to defend.

For he have slain Sir Donald Graham,
His blood lies on his sword,
And far, far distant are his men
That can't assist their lord.

Tell me where is Sir John the Ross,
I will thee well reward.
He sleeps within Lord Bohun's park,
Mathilda is his guide.

Outside the gate Mathilda stood,
To her the Graham did say:
Saw you Sir John the Ross,
Last night did he pass this way?

Last day at noon, Mathilda said,
Sir John the Ross passed by;
He spurred his steed with furious move,
'Tis onward fast did hie.

By this he's in Edinburgh
If horse and men holds good.
'Tis false, said he, your page told me
He sleeps within your wood.

SIR JAMES THE ROSS

She wrung her hands and tore her hair.
Brave Ross you are betrayed
And wounded by those means, she cried,
Of whence I hoped thine aid.

By this the gallant knight awoke,
The virgin's squeaks he heard,
And up he rose and drew his sword
As the undaunted band appeared.

Last day your sword my brother slew,
His blood yet dim with shine [it shines],
And e'er the setting of the sun,
Yours will reek on mine.

Your words are great, replied the chief,
But deeds approve the man,
Set by your band and hand to hand
We'll try what valour can.

Four of his men, the bravest four,
Fell down beneath his sword,
But still he scorned the high revenge
That sought their hearty [haughty?] lord.

Behind him beastly came the Graham
And pierced him through the side
And spurting came the purple blood.

The sad Mathilda saw him fall.
O spare his life, she cried;
Lord Bohun's daughter begs his life,
Let her not be denied.

Her loving voice the hero heard,
And raised his death-closed eyes,
And fixed them on the weeping maid
And weakly thus replied:

In vain Mathilda begs the life
Of death's arrest denied,
My race is run, adieu my love,
And closed his eyes and died.

Sung by Mrs. James Welsh at Ferryland, 1st August 1930

CHILD BALLADS

C

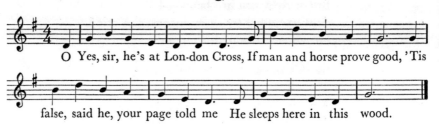

O Yes, sir, he's at Lon-don Cross, If man and horse prove good, 'Tis
false, said he, your page told me   He sleeps here in this   wood.

Sung by Mr. Bill Kennedy at Trepassey, 2nd August 1930

19 THE DOWIE DENS OF YARROW

(*The Braes o' Yarrow*)

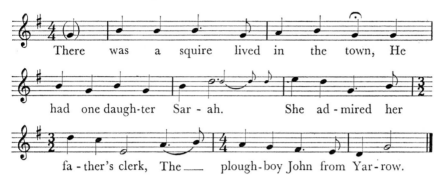

There was a squire lived in the town, He had one daugh-ter Sar - ah. She ad - mired her fa - ther's clerk, The —— plough-boy John from Yar - row.

There was a squire lived in the town,
He had one daughter Sarah.
She admired her father's clerk,
The ploughboy John from Yarrow.

As he was going up the lane,
The lane so very narrow,
And there he spied nine hired men
Waiting for his carrow.

Three he drew [withdrew?] and three he slew
And three he had slightly wounded
And her brother John stepped up behind
To pierce him bodily under.

Go home, go home, you false young man,
And tell your sister Sarah
That the prettiest flower that bloomed in June
Is the man who died in Yarrow.

She said: Brother dear, I had a dream,
I dreamed I was gathering flowers,
I dreamed I was gathering flowers
In the dewy dales of Yarrow.

Sister dear, I can read your dream
That caused you in fear to sorrow.
The sweetest flowers that bloomed in June
Is the man who died in Yarrow.

95

Her father said to her one day:
What caused you in grief to sorrow?
She threw herself in her father's arms
And she never saw tomorrow.

Sung by Mrs. May Joseph Mitchell at Marystown, Placentia Bay, 10th July
1930

20 THE GREEN WEDDING
(*Katharine Jaffray*)

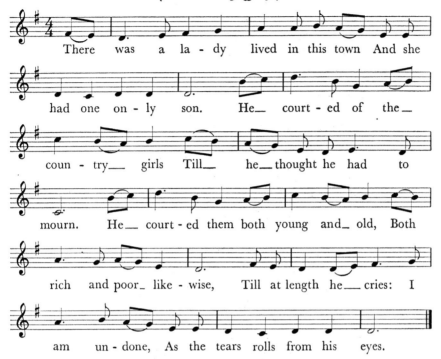

There was a la - dy lived in this town And she
had one on - ly son. He— court - ed of the—
coun - try— girls Till— he— thought he had to
mourn. He— court - ed them both young and— old, Both
rich and poor— like - wise, Till at length he— cries: I
am un - done, As the tears rolls from his eyes.

There was a lady lived in this town
And she had one only son.
He courted of the country girls
Till he thought he had to mourn.
He courted them both young and old,
Both rich and poor likewise,
Till at length he cries: I am undone,
As the tears rolls from his eyes.

She wrote her love a letter
And she signs it with her hand.
She says: I'm going to be married
Unto another man.
The very first lines he looked upon,
He smiles and this did say:
I'll deprive him of his bride
All on his wedding day.

He wrote her back an answer:
Be sure to dress in green.

G

97

A suit of the same I will put on,
At your wedding I'll be seen.
A suit of the same I will put on,
For your wedding I'll prepare,
I'll meet with you, my heart's delight,
In spite of all that's there.

His father looked at him and says:
Where have you been all day?
Or what have been the eight score men
That ride along the way?
He looked at him, he laughed at him,
He smiled and this did say:
It must have been some fairy troop
That rode along the way.

He looked east and he looked west,
And he looked all o'er the land,
Until he picked out eight score men
Belonging to the British gang.
He mounted on a milk-white steed
And a single man rode he,
And it's off to the wedding-house he has gone
All in great company.

Come fill the glass up to the brim,
Let the toast go merrily round.
Happy, happy is the man
That will enjoy the crown.
Happy, happy is the man
That will enjoy his bride.
Let another young man love her so well
As to take her from his side.

Up speaks the young bride's husband,
And a bold spoken man was he.
If it's for fighting you came here
I am the man for thee.
It's not for fighting I came here,
It's friendship for to show.
Give me one kiss from your bonny bride's lips
And away from you I'll go.

THE GREEN WEDDING

He took her round the waist so small,
And around the grass green sleeves,
It's out of the wedding-house they did go
Without any more delay.
The bands they played and the trumpets sound,
Was glorious to be seen,
And it's off to Alma Town
With his company dressed in green.

Sung by Mrs. Theresa Corbett at Conception Harbour, 23rd October 1929

21 THE LOVER'S GHOST
(*The Grey Cock*)
A

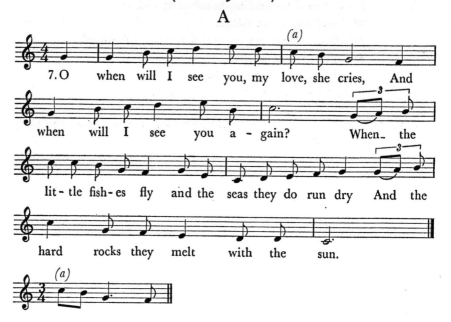

7. O when will I see you, my love, she cries, And when will I see you a - gain? When the lit - tle fish - es fly and the seas they do run dry And the hard rocks they melt with the sun.

She said unto her mamma, she said unto her dada:
There's something the matter with me,
There's something the matter and I don't know what it is,
And I'm weary from lying alone.

John he came there at the very hour appointed,
He tapped at the window so gay.
This fair maid arose and she hurried on her clothes
And let her true love John in.

She took him by the hand and on the bed she laid him,
Felt he was colder than clay.
If I had my wish and my wish it would be so,
This long night would never be morn.

Crow up, crow up, my little bird,
And don't crow before it is day,
And your cage shall be made of the glittering gold, she said,
And your doors of the silver so gay.

Where is your soft bed of down, my love,
And where is your white holland sheet,

THE LOVER'S GHOST

And where is the fair maid that watches on you
While you are taking your long silent sleep.

The sand is my soft bed of down, my love,
The sea is my white holland sheet,
And long hungry worms will feed off of me
While I'm taking my long silent sleep.

O when will I see you, my love, she cries,
And when will I see you again?
When the little fishes fly and the seas they do run dry
And the hard rocks they melt with the sun.

Sung by Mr. Matthew Aylward at Stock Cove, Bonavista Bay, 20th September
1929

B

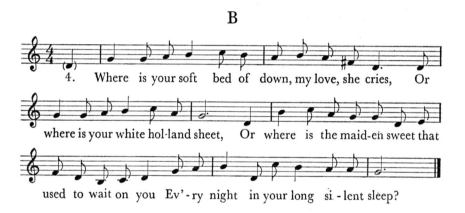

4. Where is your soft bed of down, my love, she cries, Or
where is your white hol-land sheet, Or where is the maid-en sweet that
used to wait on you Ev'-ry night in your long si-lent sleep?

Johnny is the young man that lately promised he'd marry me,
But I am afeard that he is . . .
There's something else bewailed him or else he got a charm
Or always with some fair one he's gone.

But John he come back at the very hour he appointed,
Tappen to her window so low.
The fair one then arose and hurried on her clothes
And welcomed her true love young John.

She got him by the hand and 'twas through the room she ledded him,
She felt he was colder than clay.
She says: My dearest dear, if I only had my wish,
This long night would never be day.

Where is your soft bed of down, my love, she cries,
Or where is your white holland sheet,
Or where is the maiden sweet that used to wait on you
Every night in your long silent sleep?

The sand is my soft bed of down, my love, he cries,
And the waves is my white holland sheet,
And the rocks and the worms is my jury just [*sic*] companion,
Every night I sleep in the deep.

When will I see you again, my love, she cries,
Or when will I see you any more?
When the little fishes fly and the seas will run dry
And the hard rocks will melt with the sun.

Additional stanza given 2nd October
The birds they must be false and very false, she cries,
They crow two hours too soon;
Their combs must be made of the very beads of gold
And their wings of the silver so fine.

Sung by Mr. James Day at Fortune Harbour, 1st October 1929

22 HENRY MARTIN

A

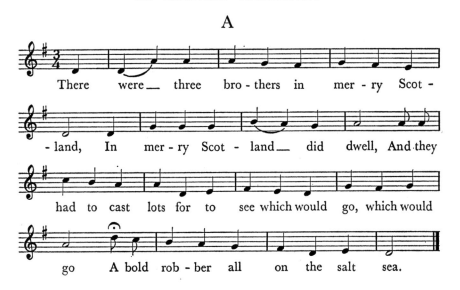

There were── three bro - thers in mer - ry Scot -
- land, In mer - ry Scot - land── did dwell, And they
had to cast lots for to see which would go, which would
go A bold rob - ber all on the salt sea.

There were three brothers in merry Scotland,
In merry Scotland did dwell,
And they had to cast lots for to see which would go, which would go
A bold robber all on the salt sea.

The nigh-est lot fell on young Henry Martin,
He being the youngest of the three;
He had to go robbing all on the salt sea, salt sea,
To maintain his two brothers and he.

He had not been sailing but a cold winter's night
Nor the part of a cold winter's day,
Before they had spied some tar-locking ship
Came a-bearing down on them so nigh.

Come rattle your main yards, cried Henry Martin,
And heave your ship under me,
For I will toss over your ball-flowing, ball-flowing boat
And your bodies I'll send to the sea.

Sung by Mr. Jos. C. Jackman at Grole, Hermitage Bay, 23rd July 1930

B

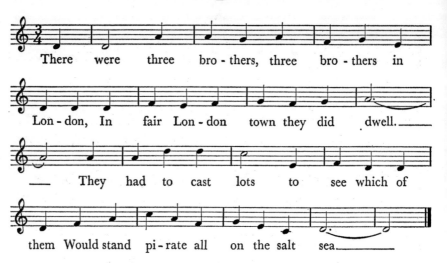

There were three brothers, three brothers in London,
In fair London town they did dwell.
They had to cast lots to see which of them
Would stand pirate all on the salt sea.

The youngest, the youngest of those brothers three,
. . . .
He had to stand pirate all on the salt sea,
For to maintain his two brothers and he.

They built them a boat and a bonny boat,
And a bonny fine boat she may be;
Her topsail was oak and her keel it was bark
And her two sides were linèd with steel.

They were not long sailing all on the sea,
At the length of a long winter's night,
And the part of a short winter's day,
When a large lofty stout ship,
A large lofty ship come rolling down on the salt sea.

What ship, what ship? cries Henry Martin,
What ship, what ship it may be?
I'm a rich merchant ship to England I'm bound,
And I pray you to let me go free.

HENRY MARTIN

Such things, such things, cries Henry Martin,
Such things that never shall be,
For your rich merchant's goods I will take on my board
And your men I'll sink in the sea.

For broadside, for broadside those two . . .
For the space of two hours or three,
Till Henry Martin gave her a broadside
And down to the bottom sank she.

Bad news, bad news, cries Henry Martin,
Bad news I have got unto thee,
Your rich merchant's goods I'm told they're all lost,
And your men are all sunk in the sea.

Sung by Mr. Patrick Bishop at Point la Hare, St. Mary's, 29th July 1930

C

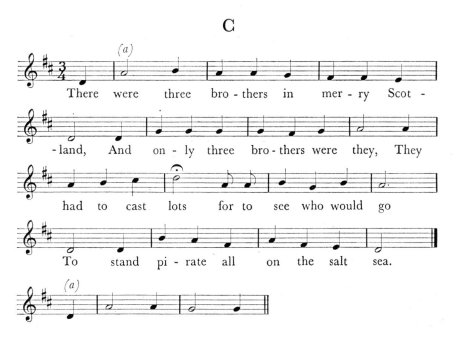

There were three brothers in merry Scotland,
And only three brothers were they,
They had to cast lots for to see who would go
To stand pirate all on the salt sea.

Hard lot did fall to Henry Martin,
The youngest of the three,

105

All for to stand pirate all on the salt sea
To maintain his two brothers and he.

He had not been sailing but a long winter's day [night]
And part of a short winter's day
When a long, lofty ship he chanced to spy
Came bearing down under our lee.

What ship, what ship? cried Henry Martin,
What ship, what ship? said he.
I'm a rich merchant ship bound for old England
If you please for to let me go free.

O no, O no, cried Henry Martin,
That thing can never be,
For I had to cast lots for to see which would go
To maintain my two brothers and me.

O throw back your main topsail and heave your ship to
And lie close up under my lee,
For your rich merchant's goods I will hoist them on board
And your mariners I'll sink in the sea.

'Twas yard-arm on yard-arm those two ships did lay,
For the space of two hours or three,
Till Henry Martin gave to her a broadside
And down to the bottom went she.

Bad news, bad news for George our King,
Bad news with a sorrowful sound,
A rich merchant's goods was taken away
And there's thirty-five mariners drowned.

Sung by Mr. John Neville at Clarke's Beach, Conception Bay, 21st October
1929

23 THE GOLDEN VANITY

The_ boy took his au - ger and ov - er board he jumped, He swam till he came to the *Gold-en Va - ni - ty,* Where he bored three holes each side, and it daz-zled all their sight, And he sank her in the low - lands, low - lands, low - lands, And he sank her in the low - lands low.

Sung by Theodore Jackman at Grole, Hermitage Bay, 22nd July 1930

24 PRETTY SALLY
(*The Brown Girl*)

A

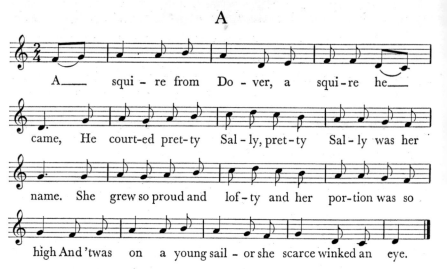

A squire from Dover, a squire he came,
He courted pretty Sally, pretty Sally was her name.
She grew so proud and lofty and her portion was so high
And 'twas on a young sailor she scarce winked an eye.

O Sally, dear Sally, O Sally dear, said he,
I'm afraid that your false heart and mine won't agree,
And if your hatred don't turn out in love,
I'm afraid that your false heart will ruin my reprove [my ruin will
prove].

. . . .
. . . . .¹

My hatred don't be to you nor to any other man,
For to say that I love you 'tis more than I can.

Six long months being over and past,
Sally, pretty Sally grew sick in love at last;
She grew sick in love and she knew not for why,
And she sent for the young man that she had once denied.

Saying: Am I the doctor that you do want to see,
Or am I the young man that you have sent for me?

¹ See Note on p. 273.

PRETTY SALLY

Yes, you are the doctor can kill or can cure,
And the pain that I do feel, my love, is hard to endure.

Can't you remember when you slighted me for scorn,
And now I will reward you for what you have done.
For what is gone and past, my love, forget and forgive,
And so spare me a little longer in this world for to live.

O yes, I might forget it, love, but never could forgive,
I will dance on your grave, my love, when you lies underneath.
She took rings from her fingers, 'twas one, two, by three
Saying: Take this, lovely Willie, in remembrance of me.
In remembrance of me, my love, when I am dead and gone,
And perhaps you might be sorry, love, for what you have done.

Sung by Mr. George Taylor at Grole, Hermitage Bay, 23rd July 1920

B

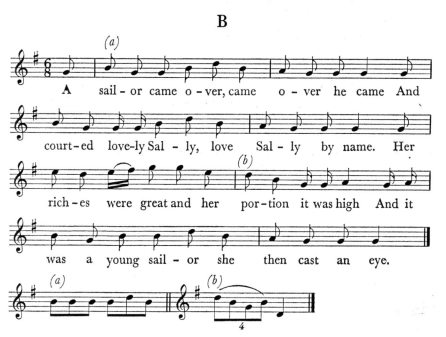

A sailor came over, came over he came
And courted lovely Sally, love Sally by name.
Her riches were great and her portion it was high,
And it was a young sailor she then cast an eye.

She got tangled into love and she knew not for why,
And she sent for the young man she once did deny.

109

Am I a doctor that you sent for me,
Or am I the young man you wish for to see?

Yes, you are the doctor can kill or can cure,
The pain I feel, my love, is hard to endure.

Where is the pain, my love, is it in your head,
Or is it in your feet?
O no dearest Willie, you have not guessed the place,
The pain that I feel, my love, lies in my breast.

Now Sally, lovely Sally, can't you remember how
You slighted me in love and you treated me with scorn,
And now I'll reward you for what you have done.

O now, dearest Willie, forget and forgive,
And spare me my life, longer to live.
O no, dearest Sally, so long as I can breathe,
I'll dance on your tomb while you lies underneath.

She pulled rings from her fingers, one, two by three,
Saying: Take these, dearest Willie, in remembrance of me
In remembrance of me, my love, when I am dead and gone,
And perhaps you may be sorrow for what you have done.

Sung by Mrs. Mary Mahoney (96) at Stock Cove, Bonavista Bay, 13th
September 1929

25 THE BLOODY GARDENER

'Twas of a la-dy fair, a— shep-herd's daugh-ter dear, She was court-ed by her own sweet-heart's de-light, But— false let-ters mo-ther wrote: Meet me dear my heart's de-light For it's a-bout some bus'-ness I have to re-late.

'Twas of a lady fair, a shepherd's daughter dear,
She was courted by her own sweetheart's delight,
But false letters mother wrote: Meet me dear my heart's delight
For it's about some business I have to relate.

O this young maid arose and to the garden goes
In hopes to meet her own true heart's delight.
She searched the ground and no true love she found,
Till at length a bloody gardener appeared in view.

He says: My lady gay, what brought you here this way,
Or have you come to rob me of my garden gay?
She cries: No thief I am, I'm in search of a young man,
Who promised that he'd meet me here this way.

Prepare, prepare, he cried, prepare to lose your life.
I'll lay your virtuous body to bleed in the ground,
And with flowers fine and gay your grave I'll overlay
In the way your virtuous body never will be found.

He took out his knife, cut the single thread of life,
And he laid her virtuous body to bleed in the ground,

And with flowers fine and gay her grave he overlaid
In the way her virtuous body never should be found.

This young man arose and into the garden goes
In hopes to meet his own true heart's delight.
He searched the garden round, but no true love he found
Till the groves and the valleys seemed with him to mourn.

O he sat down to rest on a mossy bank so sweet
Till a milk-white dove came perching round his face,
And with battering wings so sweet all around this young man's feet,
But when he arose this dove she flew away.

The dove she flew away and perched on a myrtle tree
And the young man called after her with speed.
This young man called after her with his heart filled with woe,
Until he came to where the dove she lay.

He said: My pretty dove, what makes you look so sad,
Or have you lost your love as I have mine?
When down from a tree so tall, down on her grave did fall,
She drooped her wings and shook her head and bled fresh from the
breast.

O this young man arose and unto his home did go,
Saying: Mother dear, you have me undone;
You have robbed me of my dear, my joy and my delight,
So it's alone with my darling I'll soon take flight.

Sung by Mrs. May McCabe at North River, Conception Bay, 16th October
1929

26 SHOOTING OF HIS DEAR

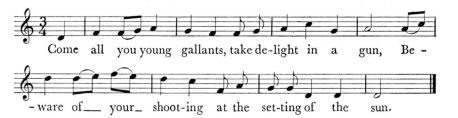

Come all you young gallants, take de-light in a gun, Be-ware of__ your__ shoot-ing at the set-ting of the sun.

Come all you young gallants, take delight in a gun,
Beware of your shooting at the setting of the sun.

As it happened one evening in a large shower of hail
In under a bower my love was concealed.

Her apron flew around her, I took her as a swan,
And I shot my own darling at the setting of the sun.

As I walked up to her I found it was she,
My limbs they grew weary and my eyes could not see

The rings on her fingers, most bitterly I cried.
O Molly, if you were living, you'd be my fond bride.

Home to my dada like lightning did run,
O father, dear father, do you know what I've done.

Her apron flew around her, I took her as a swan
And I shot my own darling at the setting of the sun.

Her apron flew around her, I took her as a swan,
And I shot my own darling, and where shall I run.

His old father in the corner with his locks turning grey:
O Jimmy, dear Jimmy don't you run away.

Only tarry in this country until your trial goes on,
You never shall be hung by the laws of the land.

O after three spaces to his uncle appears.
O Jimmy, dear Jimmy, young Jimmy is clear.

My apron flew around me, he took me as a swan,
And his heart lies a-bleeding for his own Molly Bond.

Sung by Mr. Thomas Ghaney at Colliers, Conception Bay, 22nd October
1929

27 THE CRUEL SHIP'S CARPENTER
OR
THE GOSPORT TRAGEDY

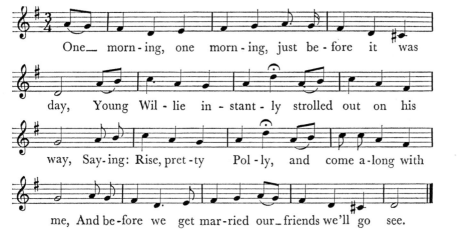

One morning, one morning, just before it was day,
Young Willie instantly strolled out on his way,
Saying: Rise, pretty Polly, and come along with me,
And before we get married our friends we'll go see.

One morning, one morning, just before it was day,
Young Willie instantly strolled out on his way,
Saying: Rise, pretty Polly, and come along with me,
And before we get married our friends we'll go see.

He led her over hills and through valleys so steep
Which caused pretty Polly to sigh and to weep,
Saying: O dearest Willie, you'll lead me astray,
And perhaps my poor innocent life to betray.

It's true, love, it's true, it's true what you say,
For this livelong night I will be digging your grave.
So they walked along together till the grave she did spy,
Which caused pretty Polly to sigh and to cry.

O pardon, O pardon, O pardon my life,
For I will not covet for to be your wife;
I'll run this world over for to set you free,
If you will but pardon my baby and me.

No pardon, no pardon, no time for to stand,
He instantly taken a knife in his hand.
He pierced her tender bosom while her heart's **blood did flow**
And into the cold grave her body did throw.

He covered her over so safe and so sound,
Not thinking this murder would ever be found.
Set sail on his own ship and ploughed the world around,
Not thinking this murder would ever be found.

And young Charlie Steward with courage so bold
One night while he's watching throughout the ship's hold,
A beautiful damsel unto him did appear
And held in her arms a baby so dear.

Our captain he summons our jolly ship's crew,
Saying: Now, my gay fellows, I fear one of you
Have murdered some fair one before we came away
And now she is haunting us here on the way.

Up speaks young Willie: I'm sure it's not me,
Up speaks another: I'm sure it's not me,
Up speaks another: I'm sure it's not me,
And those was the discussion through the ship's company.

Whoever he may be if the truth he'll deny
I'll hang him out on the yardarm so high,
And if he'll confess it his life I'll not take
I'll land him safe out on the first island I make.

O Willie was coming from the captain with speed,
He met with this fair one which caused his heart to bleed.
She ripped him, she stripped him, she tore him in three
Because he had murdered her baby and she.

She turned to the captain, those words she did say:
Since I have taken your murderer away
With the heavens' protection you and all agree
And send you safe homeward to your own country.

Sung by Miss Jemima Hincock at King's Cove, Bonavista Bay, 23rd September 1929

28 THE SEA CAPTAIN
OR
THE MAID ON THE SHORE
A

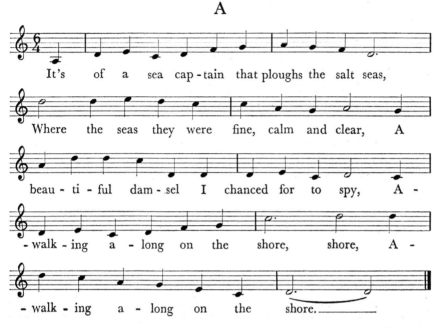

It's of a sea cap-tain that ploughs the salt seas,
Where the seas they were fine, calm and clear, A
beau - ti - ful dam - sel I chanced for to spy, A -
- walk - ing a - long on the shore, shore, A -
- walk - ing a - long on the shore.

It's of a sea captain that ploughs the salt seas,
Where the seas they were fine, calm and clear,
A beautiful damsel I chanced for to spy,
A-walking along on the shore, shore,
A-walking along on the shore.

O what will I give to my sailors so bold,
Ten guineas I vow and declare,
If you'll fetch me that lady on board of my ship,
That walks all alone on the shore *etc.*

The sailors they hoisted out a very long boat
And then to the shore they did steer,
Saying: Ma'am, if you please will you enter on board
And view a fine cargo of ware.

I have no money, the lady replied,
For to buy such costly ware.
Don't never mind that now, the sailors replied,
We'll trust you till you get on shore.

She sat herself down in the stern of the boat
And straight to the ship they did steer,
And when they arrived alongside of the ship,
The captain he ordered a chair for her,
The captain he ordered a chair.

She sat herself down in the stern of the ship
Where the seas they were fine, calm and clear.
She sang the sea-captain and his crew asleep,
And her conjuring voice didn't spare, I declare,
And her conjuring voice didn't spare.

She loaded herself up with riches so great
And all such costly wear.
The captain's broadsword she took for an oar
And she paddled away to the shore.

Sung by Mr. James Day at Fortune Harbour, 2nd October 1929

B

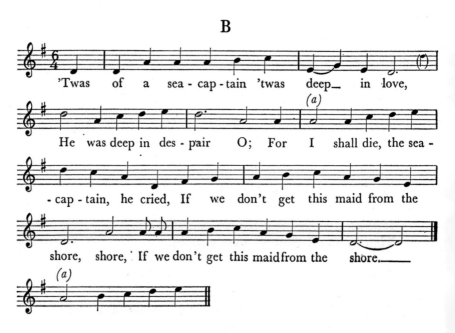

'Twas of a sea captain 'twas deep in love,
He was deep in despair O;
For I shall die, the sea captain, he cried,
If we don't get this maid from the shore, shore,
If we don't get this maid from the shore.

THE SEA CAPTAIN OR THE MAID ON SHORE

I have silver and I have gold,
I have costly ware O,
And I will buy a jolly ship's crew,
If they'll row me this maid from the shore, shore,
If they'll row me this maid from the shore.

With long persuaded they got her on boat,
The seas rose calm and clear O.
She sang so neat, so sweet and complete,
She sent sailors and captain to sleep.

She robbed them of silver, she robbed them of gold,
And robbed them of costly ware O;
She took a broad sword instead of an oar,
And paddled away for the shore.

When this man woke and found she was gone,
He was like a man in despair O.
He called up his men and commanded a boat
To row me away for the shore.

And this man's not drunk,
He's not deep in despair.
She saluted the captain as well as the crew,
Said: I am a maiden once more on the shore.

Sung by Mrs. Joanie Ryan at Stock Cove, Bonavista Bay, 18th September
1929

C

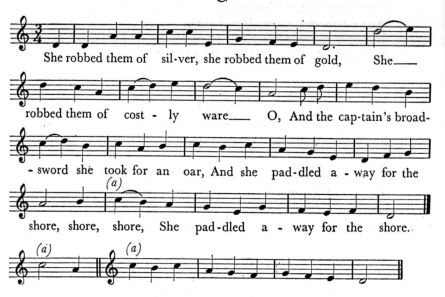

She robbed them of sil-ver, she robbed them of gold, She____ robbed them of cost-ly ware____ O, And the cap-tain's broad-sword she took for an oar, And she pad-dled a-way for the shore, shore, shore, She pad-dled a-way for the shore. (a) (a) (a)

Sung by Mrs. Isaac and Miss Stella Curtis at Trepassey, 2nd August 1930

D

It's of a fair maiden that lived on the shore,
She lived alone on the shore O.
No pleasure could find for could comfort her mind,
But she were all alone on the shore, shore, shore,
But she were all alone on the shore.

It's of a sea captain that ploughs the salt seas,
Let the wind it blow high or blow low, low,
I'll die, I'll die, the sea captain he cries,
If I don't get that maid from the shore.

I have lots of silver, I have lots of gold,
And I have lots of costly ware O,
And that I'll divide between my ship's crew
If you get me that maid from the shore.

Twenty-six seamen jumped into one boat,
Let the wind it blow high or blow low, low;
The seas were soon calm but a short change of wind,
And they soon got that maid from the shore.

THE SEA CAPTAIN OR THE MAID ON SHORE

By long persuading they got her on board,
Here's adieu to all sorrow and care O.
They gave her a seat in the cabin beneath,
Where she sat and she sang in despair.
She sang there so neat, so sweet and complete,
She sang captain and sailors to sleep.

She robbed them of silver, she robbed them of gold,
And robbed them of costly ware O.
With a captain's broadsword that she used for an oar
She paddled away to the shore.

Your men must be crazy, your men must be drunk,
Or your men must be deep in despair O
To let that fair maiden with colour so gay
Go roam all alone on the shore.

My men were not crazy, my men were not drunk,
My men were not deep in despair O.
She saluted my sailors as well as myself,
She left men in despair on the shore.

Recited by Miss Agnes Tobin at Ship's Cove, Cape Shore, Placentia, 7th
July 1930. The tune was not noted.

29 STILL GROWING

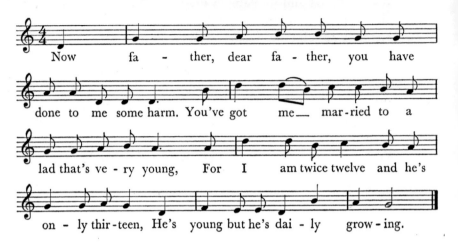

Now father, dear father, you have done to me some harm.
You've got me married to a lad that's very young,
For I am twice twelve and he's only thirteen,
He's young but he's daily growing.

O daughter, dear daughter, I have done you no wrong,
For I have got you married to a rich merchant's son,
Although you're twice twelve and he's only thirteen,
He's young, but he's daily growing.

O daughter, dear daughter, I'll tell you what we'll do,
We'll send him to the college for one year or two;
We'll tie some bonny ribbon about his bonny hair [or waist],
To let the ladies know that he's married.

As she was looking o'er her father's castle wall,
'Twas there she saw the schoolboys a-tossing of a ball,
'Twas there she saw her own true love, the flower of them all,
He's young, but he's daily growing.

Now she bought him a shirt of the old hanks of vine [sic],
She stitched it all over with her own hand,
And as she sat a-stitching the tears came rolling down,
He's young, but he's daily a-growing.

STILL GROWING

At the age of thirteen he became a married man,
At the age of fourteen his eldest son was born,
At the age of fifteen his grave was growing green,
And that put an end to his growing.

Sung by Mrs. Bridget Hall at North River, Conception Bay, 18th October
1929. The fifth stanza was given by Mrs. Mary Eller Snow.

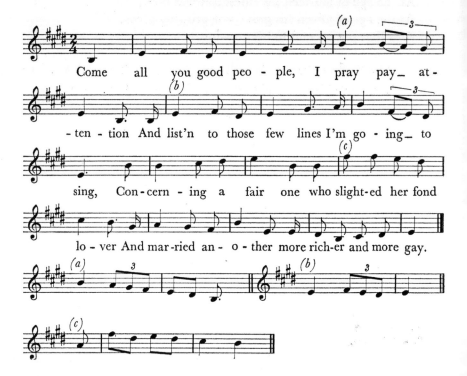

Come all you good people, I pray pay attention
And listen to those few lines I'm going to sing,
Concerning a fair one who slighted her fond lover
And married another more richer and more gay.

Now then how can you lie on another man's pillow,
When once you and I were true lovers so long,
And leave me alone to wear the green willow
And then for ever after this wide world to roam.

Now then supper was ordered and all things got ready
And the question was given O for who'd sing a song,
And the lot it did fall on her own former loved one,
The song that he sang to herself it did belong.

Now she listened to the song with the greatest of pleasure,
Verse after verse she remembered it quite well,
And to bear with those verses she could no longer listen,
It was down at the feet of the bridegroom she fell.

THE NOBLEMAN'S WEDDING

Now, she says, my dearest true love, one wish I'm going to ask you,
Hoping that you won't deny it on me.
And that is the first night to lie with my mamma
And then for ever after to lie along with thee.

Now the question that she asked him was already granted,
Sobbing and sighing she went to her bed.
Her husband rose O so early the next morning,
Went to her bedside and found she was dead.

There is a tree in my father's young garden,
Some people call it the early true bloom,
But when it bears its fruit on a cold summery morning,
It's then all false lovers will prove loyal and true.

Tune sung by Mrs. Lucy Heaney at Stock Cove, 25th September 1929. Text
sung by Mr. Mike Mahoney (brother of Mrs. Heaney) at Stock Cove, 25th
September 1929 to a tune which was very similar to that sung by Mrs. Heaney.

31 THE FALSE BRIDE
OR
SIX WEEKS BEFORE EASTER

A

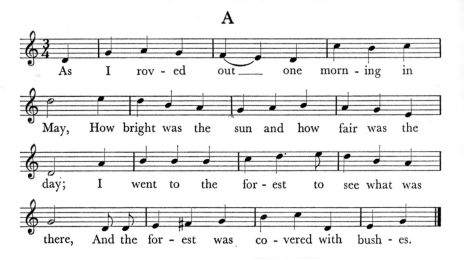

As I rovèd out one morning in May,
How bright was the sun and how fair was the day;
I went to the forest to see what was there,
And the forest was covered with bushes.

I courted a fair girl, I courted her well,
I loved that fair girl as no tongue can tell,
I loved that fair girl as I loved my own life,
And now she has gone to get married.

The first place I saw my love in the church stand,
Gold rings on her fingers, her love by the hand.
My legs they did tremble, I scarcely could stand,
To see my love wed with another.

The next place I saw my love leaving the church,
I ran out before her, I stood in the porch,
And when she passed by me I wished her much joy,
But I cursed on the man that stood by her.

The next place I saw my love sitting to eat,
I sat myself down but nothing could eat.
I said to myself: O go reason for why,
Because she is wedded to another.

THE FALSE BRIDE

The next place I saw my love in the bride's bed,
And six pretty fair maids all round her they stood.
I ran out before them, I kissed the young bride,
Saying: If I could stay there for ever.

Come dig me a grave, dig it long, wide and deep,
And cover it over with lilies so sweet,
That I may lie in it and take my last sleep,
And when I'm awake I'll forget her.

Sung by Miss Florrie Snow (16) at North River, Conception Bay, 17th October
1929

B

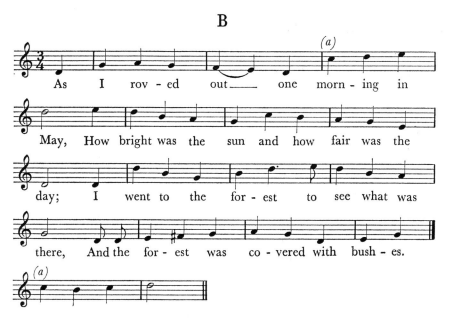

As I rov-ed out___ one morn-ing in
May, How bright was the sun and how fair was the
day; I went to the for-est to see what was
there, And the for-est was co-vered with bush-es.

Sung by Mrs. Bridget Hall at North River, Conception Bay, 18th October
1929

C

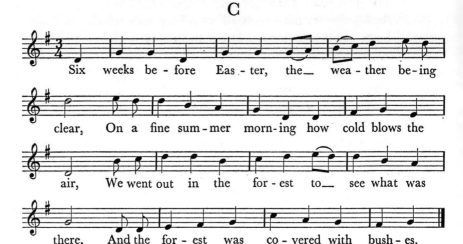

Six weeks be-fore Eas-ter, the— wea-ther be-ing clear, On a fine sum-mer morn-ing how cold blows the air, We went out in the for-est to— see what was there, And the for-est was co-vered with bush-es.

Six weeks before Easter, the weather being clear,
On a fine summer morning how cold blows the air,
We went out in the forest to see what was there,
And the forest was covered with bushes.

The bride and bride-maidens they call a grand show,
And I followed after with my heart full of woe,
And I followed after with my heart full of woe,
Saying: Here is the man who shall have her.

The first time I saw my love was in the church stand
With glove coming off and a ring putting on,
And my limbs they did tremble, I scarcely could stand,
To see my love tied to another.

Said the parson to the people: You stand out of the way
To let us hear what this young man got to say;
If this is the fair one that shall be his bride,
She shall never be tied to another.

The next time I saw my love was coming out of church,
I got off my seat and I stood in the porch.
As she passed me by I wished her much joy,
And I cursèd the man who stood by her.

The next time I saw my love she sat down to meat,
I sat myself down but nothing could eat.

THE FALSE BRIDE

I love her sweet company more better than meat
Although she was tied to another.

The next time I saw my love she was going to bed
With a store of jewels all round my love's head.
I gone in between them, I kissed the bride,
Saying: I could lie by you for ever.

Come dig me a grave both long, wide and deep
And roll it right over with lilies so sweet,
That I might lie on it and take my last sleep,
Here's adieu to false maidens for ever.

Sung by Mr. George Pearcy (Joseph) at Pass Island, 24th July 1930

32 EDWIN IN THE LOWLANDS LOW
OR
YOUNG EDMUND

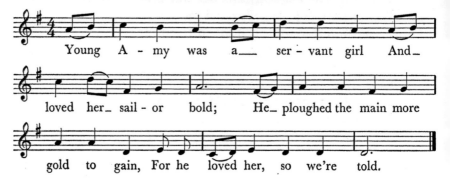

Young A - my was a__ ser - vant girl And__
loved her_ sail - or bold; He_ ploughed the main more
gold to gain, For he loved her, so we're told.

Young Amy was a servant girl
And loved her sailor bold;
He ploughed the main more gold to gain,
For he loved her, so we're told.

My father keeps a public house
Down yonder by the sea.
You must go there and venture
This night all for to stay.

Rise early in the morning.
Don't let my parents know
That your name it is young Edmund
That ploughs the lowlands low.

Young Edmund he stayed drinking
Until 'twas time to go to bed.
As little did young Edmund think
That sorrow would crown his head.

They kicked and stabbed him on the floor,
His gold they made him show,
And set his body floating
Down in the lowlands low.

Young Amy on her pillow lay,
She dreamed a dreadful dream;
She dreamed her love was murdered
And the blood did flow in streams.

EDWIN IN THE LOWLANDS LOW

Young Amy rose, put on her clothes,
And to her parents did go,
Saying: Father, dearest father,
Where's the man came here to lay?
He's dead, no tales he'll tell,
Her father this replied.

O father, dearest father,
You'll die a public show
For the murdering of my Edmund
That ploughed the lowlands low.

The shells that's in the ocean
Goes tossing to and fro,
They remind me of my Edmund
Who ploughs the lowlands low.

The fish that's in the ocean
Swim over my love's breast.
His body lies in motion,
I hope his soul's at rest.

Sung by Mrs. Curran at Conception Harbour, 23rd October 1929

33 THE THREE BUTCHERS

A

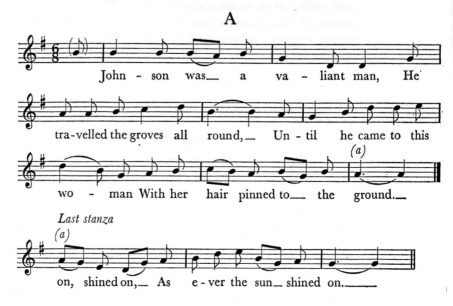

John - son was— a va - liant man, He
tra-velled the groves all round,— Un - til he came to this
(a)
wo - man With her hair pinned to— the ground.—

Last stanza
(a)

on, shined on,— As e - ver the sun— shined on.———

Johnson was a valiant man,
He travelled the groves all round,
Until he came to this woman
With her hair pinned to the ground.

What brought you here? cried Johnson,
What brought you here this way?
'Twas by ten cursèd robbers,
They have brought me here this way.

They robbèd me, they stripped me,
My hands and feet they bound.
They left me here stagnated
With my hair pinned to the ground.

Johnson was a valiant man
He took her up behind,
Taking his coat off from his back
To shelter her from the wind.

As they were riding along together
As fast as they could ride,
She put a whistle to her mouth
And gave three dismal cries.

THE THREE BUTCHERS

And out stepped ten young robbers
With weapons in their hands.
They boldly stepped to Johnson
And bid him for to stand.

I'll stand, I'll stand, cried Johnson,
As long as I can stand,
But never was I daunted
Or afraid of any man.

Out of ten nine he knocked down,
The woman he did not mind;
She drew a sword all from his side
And pierced him in behind.

This woman she was taken up,
Bound down in iron strong,
For killing of as fine a butcher man,
As ever the sun shined on, shined on,
As ever the sun shined on.

Sung by Miss Irene Barrett at Harbour Grace, 12th October 1929

B

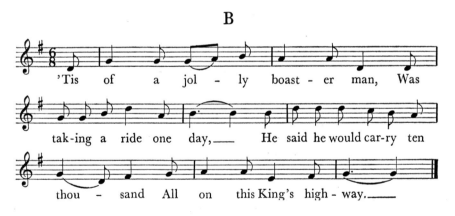

'Tis of a jol - ly boast - er man, Was tak-ing a ride one day,— He said he would car-ry ten thou - sand All on this King's high - way.——

'Tis of a jolly boaster-man,
Was taking a ride one day,
He said he would carry ten thousand
All on this King's highway.

As he was riding all alone
As fast as he could ride;

O stop, O stop, cries Johnerson,
I hear a woman cry.

He nobly turned his horse around
And looked all around,
And there he saw a woman
With her hair tied to the ground.

What brought you here? cried Johnerson,
What brought you here? he cried.
'Tis by the cursèd robbers,
They have brought me here to die.

They robbed me and they stripped me,
My hands and feet they bound,
They leaved me here stripped naked
With my hair tied to the ground.

He then got on his horseback
And took her on behind;
He put his coat off from his back
To shield her from the wind.

As they were riding all alone,
As fast as they could ride,
She put her finger to her mouth
And gave one mournful cry.

And out came out ten robbers
With weapons in their hands,
And galloped [?] up to Johnerson
And ordered him to stand.

I'll stand, I'll stand, cries Johnerson,
I'll stand as long as I can;
I was never a coward in all my life
Nor afraid of any man.

So out of ten was nine struck down,
This woman he did not mind;
She pulled her knife all from her belt
And pierced him through behind.

THE THREE BUTCHERS

I must fall, I must fall, cries Johnerson,
I must fall right to the ground;
'Tis by a wicked woman,
She has caused me my death wound.

This woman was taken up
And put in irons so strong,
For murdering one of the finest boys
That ever the sun shone on.

Sung by Miss Myrtle Parsons at Hermitage, 21st July 1930

34 THE WILDERNESS LADY

OR

A HEALTH TO THE KING

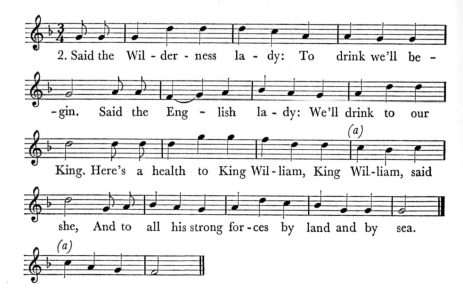

2. Said the Wil - der - ness la - dy: To drink we'll be -
-gin. Said the Eng - lish la - dy: We'll drink to our
King. Here's a health to King Wil - liam, King Wil.-liam, said
she, And to all his strong for - ces by land and by sea.
(a)

A lord's house in London, great merriment held,
Where many a rich lord and nobleman dined,
And when dinner was over, sat down to drink wine.

Said the Wilderness lady: To drink we'll begin.
Said the English lady: We'll drink to our King.
Here's a health to King William, King William, said she,
And to all his strong forces by land and by sea.

So she wrote a challenge next day in full speed,
Caused the English lady this letter to read,
When she found she challenged her broadsword to bring,
And only a-drinking a health to the king.

With broadsword and broadsword they began for to push,
When the English lady she fell in her bush [*sic*].
For bleeding and dying for mercy she cried,
Come help me I'm wounded it's here I must die.

A great lord from England rode up in full speed,
Took this young man by the waist, as he supposed him to be.

THE WILDERNESS LADY

The gold ear-rings were shining, caused them to be known,
Or else they might pass for two young men alone.

Sung by Mrs. Bridget Flanagan (80) at Avondale, Conception Bay, 25th
October 1929

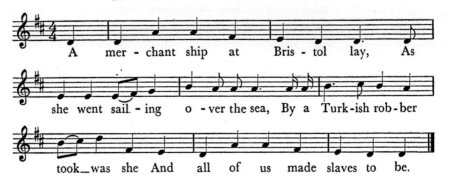

A mer - chant ship at Bris - tol lay, As she went sail - ing o - ver the sea, By a Turk-ish rob-ber took__ was she And all of us made slaves to be.

A merchant ship at Bristol lay,
As she went sailing over the sea,
By a Turkish robber took was she
And all of us made slaves to be.

They bound us down in irons strong,
And stripped and lashed us all along;
No tongue can tell, I'm certain sure,
What we poor souls now did endure.

It was my fortune for to be
A slave unto a rich lady.
She dressed herself in rich array
And went to view her slaves one day.

Hearing the moan this young man made,
She went to him and this she said:
What countryman are you, kind sir?
I am an Englishman, 'tis true.
I wish you was a Turk, said she,[1]
I'd ease you of your slavery.

O no, madam, that never can be.
Your constant slave I will always be,
But rather would I be burned to a stake,
Than ever I would my God forsake.

Then straightway to her palace went
And spent that night in discontent.
Little Cubitt with his piercèd dart
Did deeply wound her through the heart.

THE TURKISH LADY

She dressed herself in rich array
And with this young man sailed away,
And now herself turned Christian brave
And with this young man sailed away,
Which was in chains and bondage too,[1]
So this you see what love can do.

Sung by Mr. William Ball at Hermitage, 21st July 1930

[1] The last two phrases of the tune were repeated.

A

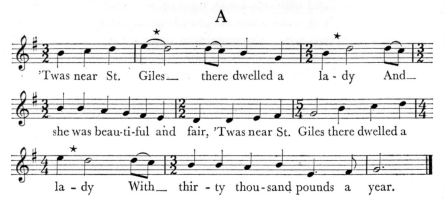

'Twas near St. Giles— there dwelled a la - dy And—
she was beau-ti-ful and fair, 'Twas near St. Giles there dwelled a
la - dy With— thir - ty thou-sand pounds a year.

The rythm of this song was very irregular and I was unable to note the exact time values. In passages marked ★ the first note of the bar was rather less than a crotchet in value.

'Twas near St. Giles there dwelled a lady
And she was beautiful and fair,
'Twas near St. Giles there dwelt a lady
With thirty thousand pounds a year.

There came to court her two loving brothers,
Not knowing their unsettled doom.
Pray come to me tomorrow morning,
Pray come to me so very soon.

And one of them was a bold sea-captain,
Commanded he was by a Colonel Gray;
The other was a bold lieutenant
On board of a Tiger's man of war.

She ordered her coaches to be got ready,
And into the town all for to go,
And there to spend one half an hour
The lions and tigers for to view.

The lions and tigers they kept such roaring,
While sat this fair one in the sun.
It was there she lay one single hour,
Quite lifeless she lay on the ground.

And when she woke and gathered her senses
Into the den she threw her fan,

THE BOLD LIEUTENANT

Saying: Where do stand that man of valour
That will fetch to me my fan again?

And then up speaks the faint-hearted captain,
Saying: You awful madam, I must refuse.
Into the den there is great danger,
I would not venture life for love.

And then up speaks the bold lieutenant,
All with a voice that sounds so high,
Saying: Here do stand the man of valour
That will fetch to you your fan or die.

Into the den he boldly ventured
Where the lions and tigers they looked so grim.
He did not seem the least undaunted,
But he looked at them so fierce again.

Now when she saw her true love coming
The least the harm to him was done,
She fold [throwed?] herself into his arms,
Saying: Take the prize, love, you have won.

Sung by Mr. Patrick Kelly at Tickle Cove, Bonavista Bay, 21st September
1929

B

In Greenock town there lived a lady
And by her beauty none could conquer.

She was so high and so condescending,
No man on earth could her husband be,
Unless it was some man of honour,[1]
Who was never conquered by land or sea.

O there was two brothers who were her lovers,
And she admired them above the rest,
And to try their valour she was intending,
To see which of them did love her the best.

Early next morning the coach got ready,
All by her orders at the break of day,
And those two brothers they both got ready,
For London Tower they rode away.

O when they came up to London Tower,
She threw her fan into the lion's den,
Saying: Which of you now will gain a lady
And bring to me back my fan again.

O then up speaks this bold sea captain,
As he stood shivering all by her side,
He said: To sea I was never daunted,
I was inclined for to serve [fight?] my foe.

But when there's wild beasts like lions and tigers
My courage to them it would prove in vain,
So now my life I'll not put in danger,
Suppose your favour I never gain.

O then up speaks the third lieutenant,
With a voice like thunder so loudly did roar;
He said: In battle I was never daunted,
I was inclined for to be in gore.

He drew his sword all from his scabbard
And boldly entered the lions' den,
And by his bold behaviour so clever
Four of the lions at his feet did fall.

O when she saw her true love coming,
No hurt nor harm unto him were done,

[1] Repeat last two lines of tune.

THE BOLD LIEUTENANT

With folded arms she did embrace him,
Saying: Here's the prize you have dearly won.

Now soon the news to the king was carried,
Saying: Four of your lions in the field is slain,
And instantly this young man was sent for
And well rewarded all for the same.

He rose him from third lieutenant
And he made him admiral all o'er the bloom [blue?]
And to his daughter that night got married.
See what the powers of love can do!

Sung by Mrs. Thomas J. Lee at Riverhead, St. Mary's, 27th July 1930

C

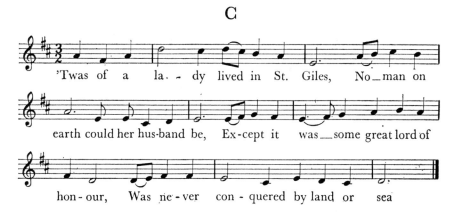

'Twas of a la - dy lived in St. Giles, No—man on
earth could her hus-band be, Ex-cept it was—some great lord of
hon-our, Was ne-ver con-quered by land or sea

'Twas of a lady lived in St. Giles,
No man on earth could her husband be,
Except it was some great lord of honour,
Was never conquered by land or sea.

There was two brothers that lived like lovers,
Who her admired more than the rest.
Then she said she would try their valiance
To see which one of them loved her best.

One of them was a bold sea-captain,
On board of a cruiser some jolly tar,
And the other of them was a third lieutenant
On board of the Tigress great man of war.

The horse and coach she then got ready,
And ordered them by the break of day,
Those two brothers being her true lovers,
For London city they drove away.

And when they drove near London city,
She threw her fan into the lions' den,
Saying: Where's that young man will gain a lady,
Take back to me my fan again.

The first that spoke was the bold sea-captain,
'Twas he stood shivering by her side:
For to face in there among lions and wild tigers
My strength to them it would prove in vain,
And I'd rather run my life in danger[1]
To spoon your favour I'll never gain.

The next that spoke was the third lieutenant
With a voice like thunder most loud to roar:
In the wars of danger sure I'm no stranger
I was oftimes choosed of a bleeding gore.

He snatched his sword down from its safeguard
And then rushed into the lions' den.
'Twas by his valiance they behaved so clever
And four of the lions at his feet they fell.

Now when the rest saw he was so clever
Down at his conqueror's feet they lay,
And then he stooped and the fan he brought her,
Unto the lady he marched away.

Now when the lady she saw him coming
And unto him no harm was done,
She gently folded her arms around him,
Saying: Take the prize, love, that you have won.

Now when her father he came to hear this,
Hearing how the lions in the den were slain,
He did not seem for to mind the matter,
But well rewarded him for the same.

[1] Repeat last two lines of tune.

THE BOLD LIEUTENANT

He raised him then from a third lieutenant
And made him an admiral of Waterloo;
Unto his daughter that night got married.
See what the powers of love can do!

Sung by Mrs. May (James) McCabe at North River, Conception Bay, 18th
October 1929

37 THE COUNCILLOR'S DAUGHTER
OR
THE LAWYER OUTWITTED

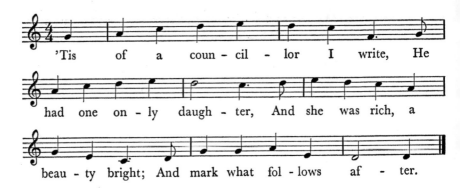

'Tis of a coun - cil - lor I write, He had one on - ly daugh - ter, And she was rich, a beau - ty bright; And mark what fol - lows af - ter.

'Tis of a councillor I write,
He had one only daughter,
And she was rich, a beauty bright;
And mark what follows after.

Her uncle left her, I declare,
A large here opposition [*sic*],
All for her father to take care
Thereat his own discretion.

Both lords and knights of a high renown,
This fair one he [they] had courted,
And more of them her favour won
So as it is reported.

Until a squire's youngest son,
He may enter her room,
And when he had her favour won
She feared 'twould prove his ruin.

You are a jewel in my eyes,
And now I fear the carressy [*sic*].
To die, I fear, will be your doom
For stealing of an heiress.

O well bespoke the young man bold,
Like a true polutation [politician?]:
146

THE COUNCILLOR'S DAUGHTER

Your father he's a councillor
We'll tell him our condition.

Ten guineas bright shall be his fee,
He'll think we are some strangers,
And for the gold he'll counsel us
And free us from all dangers.

'Twas early next morning the young man rose
To go to the lawyer's chamber,
And sure the councillor did not know
But both of them were strangers.

But when the lawyer saw the gold,
He himself to be the gainer,
A pleasant tale he told to him
Of how he could obtain her.

Do you get a horse, the councillor said,
Do you get up behind her;
She'll bring you to some neighbour's house
Where none of your friends will find her.

Then she stole you, you may declare,
And to avoid all fury,
This is law I will maintain
Before both judge and jury.

Here is my writing-hand and seal,
That seal I'll ne'er deny it;
If there's any indicting,
In court I'll stand by you.

I thank you, sir, the young man said,
By you I am befriended;
It's to your house I'll bring my wife
When all the joke is ended.

'Twas early next morning the young man rose,
The news to his dear he carried,
And she her father's counsel took
And they were safely married.

When long that night in merriment
And joy beyond expression,
And homewards they returned the next day
To ask her father's blessing.

But when the councillor saw them both,
He looked like one distracted,
And swore he'd be revenged in wrath
For what his dame had acted.

Well bespoke the young man bold,
Saying: I hope there's no indicting,
For this is law, sir, of your own,
For here is your handwriting.

O thunder nouns [*sic*], the councillor said,
Was there ever a man more fitted,
Myself to be the councillor
By you I am outwitted.

She might have lords or knights, he said,
Of higher blood descending,
But since she is your loving wife,
How can I be offended.

Here is five thousand pounds in gold
Was left her by my brother,
And when I'm dead she must have all,
For child I have no other.

Sung by Mr. Joseph O'Neill, Admiral's Cove, Fermeuse, 5th August 1930

38 JACK IN LONDON CITY
OR
JACK THE JOLLY TAR

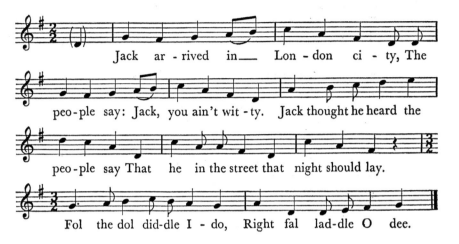

Jack ar-rived in— Lon-don ci-ty, The
peo-ple say: Jack, you ain't wit-ty. Jack thought he heard the
peo-ple say That he in the street that night should lay.
Fol the dol did-dle I-do, Right fal lad-dle O dee.

Jack arrived in London city,
The people say: Jack, you ain't witty.
Jack thought he heard the people say
That he in the street that night should lay.
    Fol the dol diddle I-do,
    Right fal laddle O dee.

To lie in the street was not Jack's fancy.
Squire walked along with lovely Nancy.
Jack thought he heard lovely Nancy say,
The squire in her arms that night should lay.

I'll tie a string to my little finger,
I'll pass the end through my room window,
And you come there and pull the string,
And I'll be down, I'll let you in.

Well, says Jack, I'm sure to venture,
I'll pull that string that hangs through the window.
And Jack went there and pulled the string
And the lady by mistake came down, let him in.

Jack got in to his heart's desire;
The lady thought Jack was the squire.

149

The squire come there and looking for the string,
And Jack was after pulling of it in.

Early in the morning the fair one woken,
She felt like one that was heart-broken,
To see Jack's tarry pants and shirt
And his face and his hands all smeared with dirt.

What brought you here, you naughty fellow,
To rob me of my virgin pillow?
Well, says Jack, I pulled the string,
And you come down and let me in.

I'll give you gold, or I'll give you money,
If you don't mention to anybody.
Well, says Jack, if I gets the gold
I'll never mention to any soul.

Jack got married to lovely Nancy;
She dressed him up quite to her fancy.
Where he treats his shipmates to rum and gin,
Saying: Damn your eyes, go pull the string.

Sung by Mr. William Holloway at King's Cove, Bonavista Bay, 20th
September 1929

39 THE RICH OLD LADY

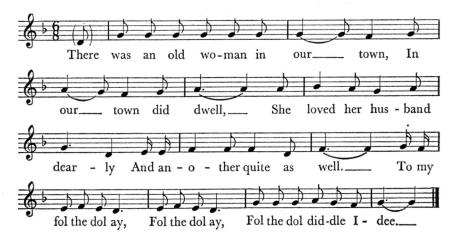

There was an old wo-man in our___ town, In our___ town did dwell,___ She loved her hus - band dear - ly And an - o - ther quite as well.___ To my fol the dol ay, Fol the dol ay, Fol the dol did-dle I - dee.___

There was an old woman in our town,
In our town did dwell,
She loved her husband dearly
And another quite as well.
 To my fol the dol ay,
 Fol the dol ay,
 Fol the dol diddle I-dee.

She went to the doctor,
To the doctor for to find,
If he'd got any medicine
To turn her husband blind.

She brought six dozen maribones,
She made him suck them all.
But now I've got the last one suck
I can't see you at all.

This old man said he would drown himself,
He did not know the way.
So come, my dear old husband,
And I'll show you the way.

'Twas hand in hand together
Down by the riverside.
This old man stepped to one side
And in she fell aright.

This old woman she struggled about
To see if she could swim.
This old man took a long stick
And pushed her farther in.

Sung by Miss Florrie Cribb at Grole, Hermitage Bay, 24th July 1930

40 THE SPANISH MAIN

I was scarce eigh - teen when I start - ed rov - ing, A pret - ty fair maid came___ in my view. When love takes place in a young man's at - ten - tion, He does not mind the hard-ships he goes through.

I was scarce eighteen when I started roving,
A pretty fair maid came in my view.
When love takes place in a young man's attention,
He does not mind the hardships he goes through.

I courted that girl for three long years,
But still her favour I could not gain.
One straight notion was my intention
That I would sail over the Spanish main.

Goodbye, darling, I'm going to leave you,
On the briny ocean to take my stand.
And it's goodbye, darling, let God be with you
And let no other sailor be at your command.

No other sailor and no tailor
Will have the privilege my heart to gain.
So goodbye, darling, and God be with you
And write to me over the Spanish main.

This poor girl she felt very lonely
A-thinking on the vows she broke,
And she felt lonely and discontented
And never a word to her mistress spoke.

They knew there was something grieved her
That very night as she went to bed,

And early next morning unto her chamber,
They found the poor girl was lying dead.

And beneath her pillow they found a letter,
'Twould grieve your banished heart full sore.
It was wet with tears and dark with kisses.
Farewell, darling, for evermore.

And the very next day was this young girl's funeral,
A letter come all in her name,
Saying: Your sailor fell from the yard-arm reefing
While sailing over the Spanish main.

This poor girl she died broken-hearted
While her sailor was killed from his work at sea.
The secrets they have got to answer
Before their Maker and the Judgement Day.

Sung by Mr. Fred Mercer (75) at Upper Island Cove, Conception Bay,
10th October 1929

41 SPANISH LADIES

Good - bye and a - dieu___ to you, Span - ish
la - dies, Good - bye and a - dieu to you, la - dies of
Spain, For we've re - ceived or - ders to run to old
Eng - land, Hop - ing in___ short time___ to see you a - gain.

Goodbye and adieu to you, Spanish ladies,
Goodbye and adieu to you, ladies of Spain,
For we've received orders to run to old England,
Hoping in short time to see you again.
 We'll rant and we'll roar like true British sailors,
 We'll rant and we'll roar across the salt seas,
 Until we strike soundage in the Channel of old England,
 From England to Sweden is ninety-five leagues.

We'll round our ship to and the wind at sou'west, boys,
We'll round our ship to for to strike soundage clear.
Our lead it strikes bottom in ninety-five fathoms,
Then we ran our main-yards, up channel did steer.

The first land we sighted was the Philadelphee,
The next we sighted was the Island of Wight;
We sailèd then by Beaches, to the Isle of Wight at Dungeon,
And then bore away for South Portal light.

The signal was given by the grand fleet to anchor,
All in the Downs that night for to lie.
Stand by your ring stopper, see clear your shank painter,
Ease up your clew garnets, stand by tacks and sheets.

SEA SONGS

Now let each tar drink a full flowing bumper,
And let each tar drink a full flowing bowl;
We'll drink and be merry and drown melancholy.
Here's adieu to all fair mates and Sarah so bold.

Sung by Mr. James Day at Fortune Harbour, 2nd October 1929

42 THE GREENLAND FISHERY

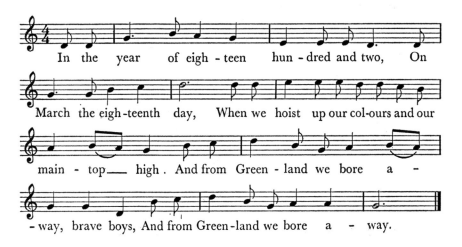

In the year of eigh - teen hun - dred and two, On
March the eigh - teenth day, When we hoist up our col - ours and our
main - top__ high . And from Green - land we bore a -
- way, brave boys, And from Green - land we bore a - way.

In the year of eighteen hundred and two,
On March the eighteenth day,
When we hoist up our colours and our main-top high
And from Greenland we bore away, brave boys,
And from Greenland we bore away.

And when we reached that barren place
Where yonder grows no green,
Where the cold frost and snow and the whale fish blow
And the daylight was seldom seen, brave boys,
And the daylight was seldom seen.

Our captain walking the quarter-deck,
And a gallant man was he,
Saying: Boys, overhaul, let your Davit tackles fall
And launch out your boats all three, *etc.*

The bosun went to the main-top high
With a spy-glass in his hand.
A whale, a whale, a whale fish, he cries,
And he blows on our starboard bows, *etc.*

Our boat were lowered and our lines got in,
And every man in view,
And every man was determined for to watch,
For to watch where the whale fish blew, *etc.*

SEA SONGS

We struck the whale and our lines played out,
And he gave us a slap of his tail,
And he upset the boat and we lost five men,
And we never could kill that Greenland whale, *etc.*

Sad news, sad news to our captain brought,
Of the loss of five men,
Likewise the loss of that Greenland whale,
Which grieves me ten times more, *etc.*

I'd be by my fond mother's side[1]
And the pretty girls on the shore,[1]
In the year of eighteen hundred and two,
And March the eighteenth day,
And from Greenland we bore away, brave boys,
And from Greenland we bore away.

Sung by Miss Mary Ryan at Riverhead, St. Mary's, 28th July 1930

---

[1] These lines would seem to be an intrusion.

Transposed Mixolydian

The Drowned Lover

43 SWEET WILLIAM

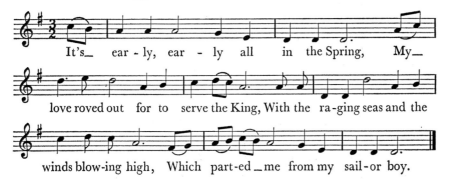

It's_ ear-ly, ear-ly all in the Spring, My_ love roved out for to serve the King, With the ra-ging seas and the winds blow-ing high, Which part-ed_me from my sail-or boy.

It's early, early all in the Spring,
My love roved out for to serve the King,
With the raging seas and the winds blowing high,
Which parted me from my sailor boy.

O father, father, build me a boat,
And it's on the ocean I'll go float,
And I'll hail the ships as they pass me by
Until I get news from my sailor boy.

She had not long been over the sea,
When a man-of-war ship she chanced to see.
O captain, captain, come tell me true,
Did my love Willie sail on board with you?

What kind of a lad is your Willie dear?
What kind of clothing did your Willie wear?
He wears a jacket of the royal blue,
And it's easily seen that his heart is true.

O the colour of amber is my love's hair,
His cherry cheeks sets my heart in snare,
His ruby lips so soft and fine,
It's often times he pressed them to mine.

O no, fair maid, he is not here,
Your Willie is drownèd I greatly fear,
For the last green island as we passed by,
I lost four more and your sailor boy.

THE DROWNED LOVER

She wrung her hands and tore her hair
Just like some girl in deep despair.
From the captain's deck to the main top high
Let ye mourn black for my sailor boy.

She wrote a letter and she wrote it long,
And in the middle she wrote a song,
And every line she shed a tear,
And every verse she cries: Willie dear.

Come dig me my grave both wide and deep,
Place a marble tombstone to my head and feet,
And in the middle put a turtle dove
To let the world know that I died of love.

Sung by Mrs. Curran at Conception Harbour, 28th October 1929

44 ARBOUR TOWN

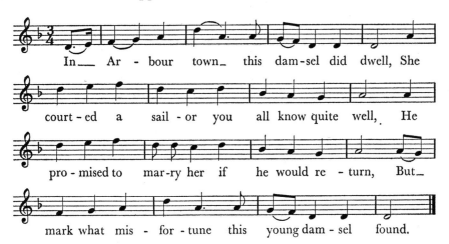

In__ Ar - bour town__ this dam-sel did dwell, She
court - ed a sail - or you all know quite well, He
pro - mised to mar-ry her if he would re - turn, But__
mark what mis - for - tune this young dam - sel found.

In Arbour town this damsel did dwell,
She courted a sailor you all know quite well,
He promised to marry her if he would return,
But mark what misfortune this young damsel found.

He had not been sailing long across this sea
Before deep heavy clouds rose to darken the sky,
When the winds they did rise and the billows did roar,
Caused many a poor sailor to lie on the lee shore.

Some they had sweethearts and more they had wives.
This unfortunate young man he swum for his life,
And out of the number he chanced for to be one,
He lost his sweet life in the watery tomb.

When the sad news came to Arbour town,
This beautiful damsel her head she hung down,
Saying: There's adieu to all sorrow since my joys they are fled,
There's a funeral instead of a marriage bed.

As she was a-walking alone on the strand,
A-tearing her hair and wringing her hands,
Saying: Cry, cruel waves, wash my true love on shore,
That I may behold his fond features once more.

As she was a-walking alone on the strand,
When first she saw Jimmie amazed she did stand,

THE DROWNED LOVER

When first she saw Jimmie amazed she did stand,
She knew it was her true love by the mark on his hand.

She kissed him and hugged him ten thousand times o'er,
Saying: Now I have got you once more on the shore,
And now I'm quite willing to lie by his side,
And a few moments after this fair one she died.

In Arbour churchyard they buried them there,
And down on the headstone large letters wrote fair:
Come all constant lovers as ye do pass by
And pray you take warning how this young couple died.

Sung by Mrs. Bridget Hall at North River, Conception Bay, 16th October
1929

45 REILLY THE FISHERMAN

As I roved out one _ e-ven-ing down · by a_ ri-ver-
-side, I_ spied a_ love-ly_ fair maid as the tears fell from her
eyes. This is a_ cold and storm-y night, these words she then did
say: My love is_ on the _ ra-ging sea, bound to A-mer-i-kee.

As I roved out one evening down by a riverside,
I spied a lovely fair maid as the tears fell from her eyes.
This is a cold and stormy night, these words she then did say:
My love is on the raging sea, bound to Amerikee.

My love he was a fisherman, his age was scarce eighteen;
He was as smart a young man as ever yet was seen.
My father he had riches great and Reilly he was poor;
Because I loved that fisherman he could not me endure.

John O'Reilly was my true love's name, lived near the town of Bray.
My mother took me by the hand, these words to me did say:
If you are fond of Reilly you must quit his company,
For your father swears he'll take his life, so shun his company.

O mother dear, now don't be severe. Where will you send my love?
For my very heart lies in his breast as constant as a dove.
O daughter dear, I'm not severe; here is one thousand pounds.
Send Reilly to Amerikee and purchase there some land.

When Ellen got the money, to Reilly she did run,
Says: This very night to take your life my father charged the gun,
Saying: Here's one thousand pounds in gold my mother sent to you,
So sail away to Amerikay and I will follow you.

He was not long a-sailing, a-sailing along the shore,
When Reilly he came back again to take his love on board.

THE DROWNED LOVER

The ship was wrecked, all hands were lost, and her father grieved full
sore
To see John Reilly in her arms as she drowned upon the shore.

'Twas in her bosom a note was found and it was wrote in blood,
Saying: Cruel must my father be when he tried to shoot my love.
So let this now be a warning to all fair maids so gay;
Don't never let the lad you love sail to Amerikay.

Sung by Miss Mary Gallahue at Stock Cove, Bonavista Bay, 20th September
1929

46 THE SIMPLE PLOUGHBOY

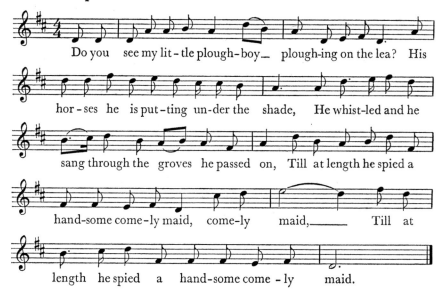

Do you see my lit-tle plough-boy— plough-ing on the lea? His hor-ses he is put-ting un-der the shade, He whist-led and he sang through the groves he passed on, Till at length he spied a hand-some come-ly maid, come-ly maid,_____ Till at length he spied a hand-some come-ly maid.

Do you see my little ploughboy ploughing on the lea?
His horses he is putting under the shade,
He whistled and he sang through the groves he passed on,
Till at length he spied a handsome comely maid, comely maid,
Till at length he spied a handsome comely maid.

When her old father did come for to know
Her ploughboy were ploughing on the lea,
He sent a bold press-gang and he pressed her love away
And he sent him to the war to be slain, *etc.*

With jacket and trousers this damsel she put on,
Two pockets were lined with gold.
She walked down the street and the pumps were on her feet
And she passed for a jolly sailor bold.

The first man she met being a jolly sailor bold,
Did you see my little ploughboy on the way?
Your ploughboy's on the deep, he's going to join the fleet,
And he said: My comely maid will you and I?

She stepped on board and he rowed her to the ship;
To the captain she made her complaint.

THE FEMALE SAILOR BOY

Our captain sighed and said: Step on shore, my comely maid,
For we're going to the wars to be slain.

She put her hands into her pocket, she took out handfuls of gold,
Five hundred bright guineas or more.
She throwed it on the deck, took her true love round the neck;
She kissed him, she brought him to the shore.

Now they're on the shore, where they've often been before,
Marriagement and joyment they'll bring.
The joy-bells did ring and the pretty birds did sing,
She got married to the young man she adored.

Curse be on the deep caused many a girl to weep,
And many to see their own true love no more.
But happy is the bride with her true love by her side;
She can see that her troubles is all o'er.

Sung by Mr. Alex Wells at Exploits, Notre Dame Bay, 5th October 1929

47 THE PRESS GANG

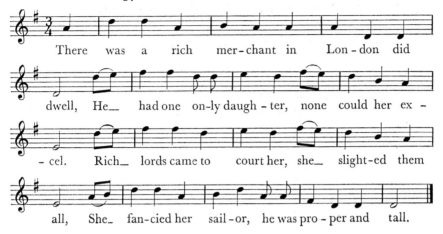

There was a rich mer-chant in Lon-don did dwell, He_ had one on-ly daugh-ter, none could her ex- -cel. Rich_ lords came to court her, she_ slight-ed them all, She_ fan-cied her sail-or, he was pro-per and tall.

There was a rich merchant in London did dwell,
He had one only daughter, none could her excel.
Rich lords came to court her, she slighted them all,
She fancied her sailor, he was proper and tall.

When her old father came this for to hear,
'Twas on her love William his vengeance did swear:
You can get better matches your arms to embrace
Than to marry a sailor your friends to disgrace.

O pardon me, father, O pardon me, sir,
There is none in this world but a sailor for me;
A sailor's my true love and I'll be his bride,
If I don't gain him my life I'd destroy.

What, what, cried her father, what, what, he did say,
You must court him in private and speak not of me,
And when all things is ready I'll surely agree.

As the lady and the sailor walked by the sea-shore,
The press-gang surrounded him and half a score more.
They pressed my own true love and they tore him from me,
Instead of great mirth 'twas a sorrowful day.

This lady she dressed herself up in men's clothes,
Straightway to the captain she immediately goes.
She signed as a sailor and it fell to her lot
To lie with her true love, but he knew her not.

THE FEMALE SAILOR BOY

As the lady and the sailor was ploughing the deep,
Said the lady to the sailor: You sigh in your sleep.
I once had a true love, the sailor did say,
'Twas by her cruel father I was sent away.

I am an astrologer, brought up by my pen,
Astrologer's books I do read now and then.
If you tell me your name I'll cast out your lot
And see if you'll gain that fair lady or not.

He told her his name and the hour of his birth.
She says: You were born for right joy and mirth;
You shall gain this fair one in spite of them all,
So here is your Ellen just now at your call.

This couple got married before the ship's crew
Which proves this fair damsel to be constant and true;
And they're now sailing over to old England's fair shore
And here's a fig for her old father she'll never see more.

Sung by Mr. William Malloy at St. Shotts, St. Mary's Bay, 3rd August 1930

48 WEARING OF THE BLUE

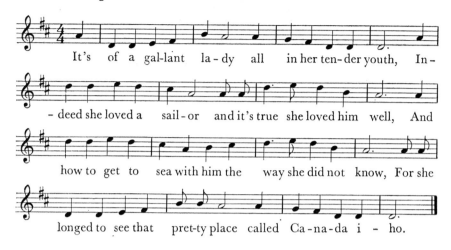

It's of a gallant lady all in her tender youth,
Indeed she loved a sailor and it's true she loved him well,
And how to get to sea with him the way she did not know,
For she longed to see that pretty place called Canada i-ho.

She bargained with a sailor lad all for a purse of gold,
And straightway he led her down in the ship below,
Saying: I'll dress you up in sailor's clothes and the colour shall be blue,
And you soon shall see that pretty place called Canada i-ho.

And when her true love heard of this he flew into a rage,
And all the whole ship's company was willing to engage,
Saying: I'll tie my love both hands and feet, it's overboard she'll go,
And she never will see that pretty place called Canada i-ho.

Then up speaks the captain: Such things will never be,
For if you drown that pretty girl all hangèd we shall be.
I'll dress you up in sailor's clothes and the colour shall be blue,
And you soon will see that pretty place called Canada i-ho.

They hadn't been in Canada no more than half a year
Before the captain married her and callèd her his dear.
She's dressed in silks and satin and she calls a gallant show,
She's the finest captain's lady in Canada i-ho.

Come all you fair young maidens where'er that you be,
Be sure to follow your true love if he is on the sea,

THE FEMALE SAILOR BOY

For if the mate he did prove false the captain he proved true,
And you see what honour I have gained by wearing of the blue.

Sung by Mr. Clarence Coffin at Rencontre, Fortune Bay, 8th July 1930

49 WILLIAM TAYLOR

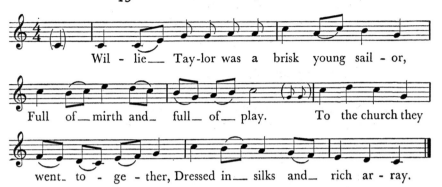

Wil - lie— Tay-lor was a brisk young sail - or,
Full of— mirth and— full— of— play. To the church they
went— to - ge - ther, Dressed in— silks and— rich ar - ray.

Willie Taylor was a brisk young sailor,
Full of mirth and full of play.
To the church they went together,
Dressed in silks and rich array.

The bells were ringing, the birds were singing,
To the church they went straightway.
In come twenty brisk young sailors,
Pressed my Willie far from me.

A short time after this fair one followed,
Went in the name of rich apparel,[1]
With her soft hands and splendid fingers
All to endure pitch and tar.

Now she is on the main-yard reefing,
Doing her duty among the rest.
As soon as her waistcoat did blow open
The captain saw her lily-white breast.

As soon as the captain came to see it,
What misfortunes have brought you here?
I'm in the search of my own true lover,
He who first I loved so dear.

Are you in search of your own true lover?
Tell to me his name, I pray.
Some do call him Willie Taylor,
Seven long years he has gone from me [away?].

[1] 'Man's apparel she did wear.'

171

THE FEMALE SAILOR BOY

You should rise early next morning,
This in honour of break of day,
There you'll see young Willie Taylor
Exporting [sporting?] with his lady gay.

A case of pistols she did call for,
They were already granted at her command.
She fired and shot young Willie Taylor,
Standing with his bride at his right hand.

As soon as the captain came to hear it,
What misfortune have you done?
I'll make you my first lieutenant
Of a ship nine hundred tons.

Now she's on the ocean sailing,
And sailing with her broadsword in hand,
And every time she makes a motion
They do tremble at her command.

Sung by Mrs. James Day at Fortune Harbour, Notre Dame Bay, 1st October
1929

50 THE ROSE OF BRITAIN'S ISLE

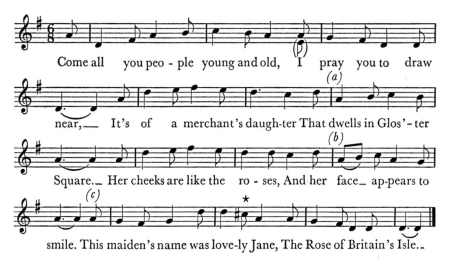

Come all you peo - ple young and old, I pray you to draw
(a)
near,— It's of a merchant's daugh-ter That dwells in Glos'-ter
(b)
Square.— Her cheeks are like the ro - ses, And her face— ap-pears to
(c) *
smile. This maiden's name was love-ly Jane, The Rose of Britain's Isle.—

(a) *(b)*

(c)

★ Sung slightly flat.

Come all you people young and old,
I pray you to draw near,
It's of a merchant's daughter
That dwells in Gloucester Square.
Her cheeks are like the roses,
And her face appears to smile.
This maiden's name was lovely Jane,
The Rose of Britain's Isle.

She was a merchant's daughter,
Her father's only joy,
Until she fell in love with
Her father's prentice boy.
His cheeks were like the roses,
And his face appears to smile.
By all above he swore he'd love
The Rose of Britain's Isle.

173

THE FEMALE SAILOR BOY

When her old agèd father heard
That he was courting her,
He wrung his hands and tore his hair,
Most bitterly did swear,
Saying: Before you'll bring disgrace on me
I'll send you many a mile
With great disdain across the main
From the Rose of Britain's Isle.

Young Edwin went on board the ship
For to cross over the main,
While Jane alone in anguish moaned,
Her bosom heaved with pain.
She dressed herself in man's attire
And after a little while
On board the ship with young Edwin went
The Rose of Britain's Isle.

When they were crossing the coasts of Spain
The enemy gave alarm.
'Twas by a ball young Jane did fall
And wounded her right arm.
The sailors ran to lend a hand
While Edwin in action smile.[1]
The sailors swore by all on board
'Twas the Rose of Britain's Isle.

Young Edwin he being thunderstruck,
His heart was filled with pain.
As soon as Jane recovered
They sailed back across the main;
As soon as Jane recovered
And after a little while,
Back home again with Edwin gay,
The Rose of Britain's Isle.

Her father he being dead and gone,
Now joys are to relate,
He willed a handsome fortune
Likewise a large estate.

[1] 'While Jane on them did smile' in other versions.

THE ROSE OF BRITAIN'S ISLE

And after a little while
Young Edwin he made Jane his bride [*bis*]
The Rose of Britain's Isle.

Sung by Mrs. Lizzie Mahoney at Stock Cove, Bonavista Bay, 25th September
1929

The Lover's Farewell and Absence

51 FAREWELL NANCY

A

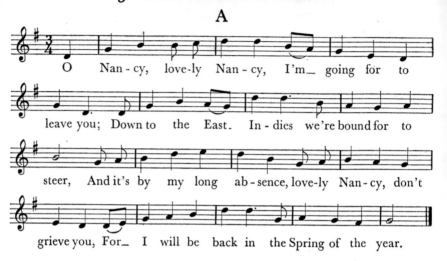

O Nan-cy, love-ly Nan-cy, I'm_ going for to
leave you; Down to the East_ In-dies we're bound for to
steer, And it's by my long ab-sence, love-ly Nan-cy, don't
grieve you, For_ I will be back in the Spring of the year.

O Nancy, lovely Nancy, I'm going for to leave you;
Down to the East Indies we're bound for to steer,
And it's by my long absence, lovely Nancy, don't grieve you,
For I will be back in the Spring of the year.

O Willie, lovely Willie, shall I go along with you?
In the midst of all danger with you I shan't fail;
When the cold stormy winds, love, and the hurricanes are blowing,
My dear, I shall be ready to reef your topsail.

It's not your little fingers our cables can't handle
And your neat little feet our topsail can't go;
When the cold stormy winds, love, and the hurricanes are blowing;
I will advise you, lovely Nancy, to the seas do not go.

Where Willie was sailing and Nancy kept waving,
Her cheeks being more paler than ever was before;
With her gold gay locks, love, she tenderly kept tearing of,
You are gone, lovely Willie, where I'll see you no more.

Come all you young maidens, by me take warning,
Don't never love a sailor that sails o'er the main.
For today they will court and tomorrow they will slight you,
And they'll leave you in sorrow, in grief to complain.

Sung by Mrs. Alice Sims at Pass Island, 24th July 1930

FAREWELL NANCY

B

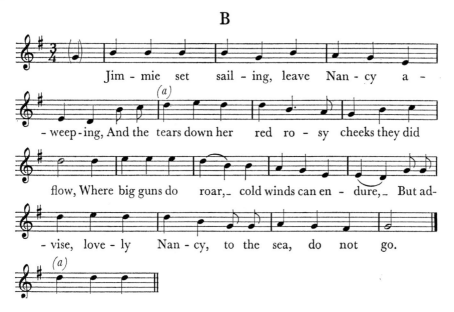

Jim - mie set sail - ing, leave Nan - cy a -
- weep-ing, And the tears down her red ro - sy cheeks they did
flow, Where big guns do roar,_ cold winds can en - dure,_ But ad-
- vise, love - ly Nan - cy, to the sea, do not go.

Jimmie set sailing, leave Nancy a-weeping,
And the tears down her red rosy cheeks they did flow,
Where big guns do roar, cold winds can endure,
But advise, lovely Nancy, to the sea, do not go.

I'll dress as a sailor and with you I'll wander,
For it's to the East Indies we're bound for to steer,
Where big guns do roar, cold winds can endure,
But advise, lovely Nancy, to the sea, do not go.

Your dear little fingers cold cables can't handle,
Your dear little toes to the main-top can't go,
Your delicate body cold winds can't endure,
But advise, lovely Nancy, to the sea, do not go.

Sung by Mrs. Bridget Hall at North River, Conception Bay, 18th October
1929

52 JIMMY AND NANCY

OR

LISBON

A

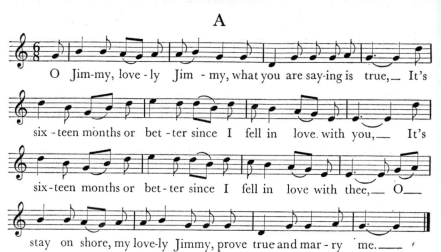

O Jim-my, love-ly Jim - my, what you are say-ing is true,— It's
six -teen months or bet -ter since I fell in love. with you,— It's
six-teen months or bet- ter since I fell in love with thee,— O—
stay on shore, my love-ly Jimmy, prove true and mar - ry me.—

O Jimmy, lovely Jimmy, what you are saying is true,
It's sixteen months or better since I fell in love with you,
It's sixteen months or better since I fell in love with thee,
O stay on shore, my lovely Jimmy, prove true and marry me.

If I should stay on shore, my love, some other would take my place,
And that would be a scandal, love, likewise a deep disgrace.
The Queen has ordered for seamen bold and I for one must go,
All for my life this very night, love, I should not answer No.

I will cut off my yellow locks, men's clothing I'll put on,
And I will go along with you to be your waiting man.
Perhaps in battle you may be when you may raise a ball,
I'll bandage up your bleeding wounds, love, I will be at your call.

Your waist it is too slender, love, your fingers they are too small,
To wait on you in battle upon you I will call,
Where big guns loud do rattle and a musket ball do fly.
The silver trumpet shall sound, my love, to drown all dismal cry.

If I should meet some other girl, so bonny, brisk and gay,
If I should fall in love with her, what would my Nancy say?
What would your Nancy say, Jimmy, sure she would like her too,
She'd gently step on one side when she'd be kissing you.

JIMMY AND NANCY or LISBON

O Nancy, my lovely Nancy, those words have gone to my heart,
This night we will get married and that before we part.
This night we will get married riding safe over the main.
God send us safe returns again, my own dear soldier maid.

Sung by Mrs. Bridget Hall at North River, Conception Bay, 19th October
1929

B

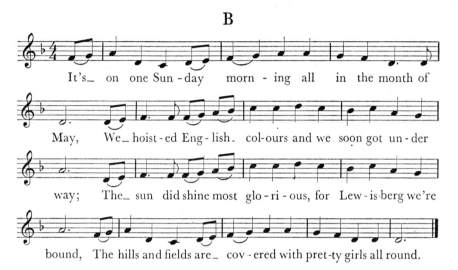

It's_ on one Sun-day morn-ing all in the month of
May, We_ hoist-ed Eng-lish. col-ours and we soon got un-der
way; The_ sun did shine most glo-ri-ous, for Lew-is-berg we're
bound, The hills and fields are_ cov-ered with pret-ty girls all round.

It's on one Sunday morning all in the month of May,
We hoisted English colours and we soon got under way;
The sun did shine most glorious, for Lewisberg we're bound,
The hills and fields are covered with pretty girls all round.

Don't you say so, dear Willie, those words it breaks my heart.
Let you and I get married this night before we part.
For the king hath wrote for seamen boys and I for one must go,
And on your virgin life, my dear, I can't say No.

My yellow locks I will cut off, man's apparel I'll put on,
And I will go along with you and be your servant man,
And when your watch it is on deck your duty I will do,
Or on the fields of battle, my love, I'll attend on you.

O no, your pretty little fingers, love, they are too slight and small,
Your waist it is too slender to face those cannon balls.
The cannon balls do rattle and silver then do fly,
And the silvery trumpets around me do drown all dismal cries.

Sung by Mrs. Janie Augot at Rencontre, Fortune Bay, 18th July 1930
179

53 NANCY OF LONDON

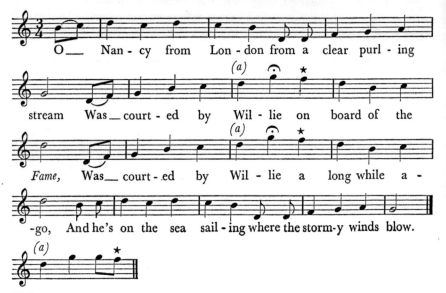

O__ Nan - cy from Lon - don from a clear purl - ing
stream Was__ court - ed by Wil - lie on board of the
Fame, Was__ court - ed by Wil - lie a long while a -
-go, And he's on the sea sail - ing where the storm-y winds blow.

★ There was a tendency to sharpen this note, more particularly when the variant
was sung.

O Nancy from London from a clear purling stream
Was courted by Willie on board of the *Fame*,
Was courted by Willie a long while ago,
And he's on the sea sailing where the stormy winds blow.

The stormy winds blow, love, makes my heart to ache,
Causes my parlour window to shiver and shake.
God knows where my love lies, he's far from the shore
And I'll pray for his safety. What can I do more?

A ship on the ocean it's a wonderful sight,
Like an army of soldiers just going to fight,
But a soldier can lay down his fire-arms and run,
While a seaman must yield to a watery tomb.

When seamen go drinking, drink the health to their wives;
Young men love their sweethearts as they love their lives,
And the health bowl goes round with a full glass in hand.
Here's a health to loving Nancy we left on dry land.

Green grow the rushes o'er the tops of them small [or all],
My love it's a peril that will grow o'er them all.

NANCY OF LONDON

The green leaf will wither and the root will decay,
And the red rose will flourish when my love comes from sea.

Sung by Mr. Samuel Moss at Open Hall, Bonavista Bay, 21st September
1929

54 THE WINTER'S GONE AND PAST

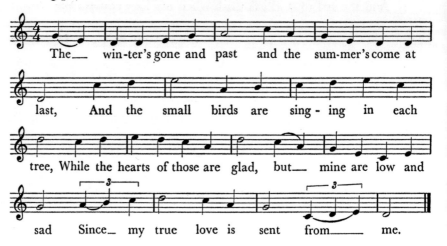

The winter's gone and past and the summer's come at last,
And the small birds are singing in each tree,
While the hearts of those are glad, but mine are low and sad
Since my true love is sent from me.

I'll put on a cap of black and bind chains around my neck
And gold rings on my fingers I'll wear.
All this I'll undertake for my own true lover's sake,
For he drives near the Carrow of Kildare.

The ivory I will wear and I'll comb down my hair
And I'll dress in the velvet so green.
Straightway I will prepare for the Carrow of Kildare
And it's there I will gain tidings of him.

My love is like the sun in the firments [firmament] did run,
He's always both constant and true;
But yours are like the one that rages up and down,
Every one in the year is as now.

Now all that is in love and the pain can't remove,
Will you pity the ardours by me.
I'm here in iron chains and obliged to remain
Since my true love is absent from me.

Farewell, my joy and heart, then since you and I must part,
Here's the first I ever did see.

THE WINTER'S GONE AND PAST

I never was inclined for to alter my mind
Although you're below my degree.

Sung by Mrs. Elizabeth Farrell at Beaubois, Placentia Bay, 11th July 1930

The Returned Lover

55 THE DARK-EYED SAILOR

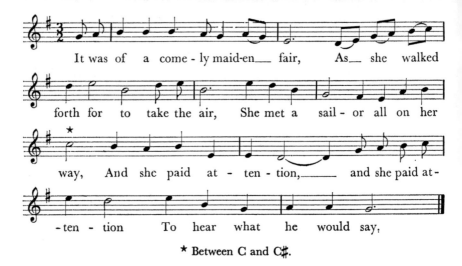

It was of a come-ly maid-en__ fair, As__ she walked forth for to take the air, She met a sail-or all on her way, And she paid at-ten-tion,_____ and she paid at--ten-tion To hear what he would say.

* Between C and C♯.

It was of a comely maiden fair,
As she walked forth for to take the air,
She met a sailor all on her way,
And she paid attention, and she paid attention
To hear what he would say.

He says: Fair maid, why do you roam?
The days have gone and the night coming on.
She says, while tears from her eyes did flow:
For my dark-eyed sailor, for my dark-eyed sailor,
So manly, stout and bold.

He says: Fair maid, drive him from your mind.
Some other sailor so good you will find.
She drove a sigh and so pale did grow,
Like a winter's morning, like a winter's morning,
When the hills are covered with snow.

His dear blue eyes and his curly hair,
His rosy cheeks have my heart ensnared.
He is genteel, not a rake like you,
And I refuse to slight, and I refuse to slight
His jacket blue.

184

THE DARK-EYED SAILOR

Seven years since he left the land,
He took the gold ring from off his hand,
He broke the token, left half with me
While the other lies rolling, while the other lies rolling
In the bottom of the sea.

It was then the token young Willie showed.
She felt distracted with joy and woe.
You're welcome, Willie, I have land and gold;
For my dark-eyed sailor, for my dark-eyed sailor
A maid I'd live and die.

It was in a cot down by the sea,
Join hands in wedlock they did agree,
Saying: Girls, be true while your love's away,
For a cloudy morning, for a cloudy morning
Brings forth a pleasant day.

Sung by Mrs. Theresa Corbett at Conception Harbour, 24th October 1929

56 THE PRIDE OF GLENCOE

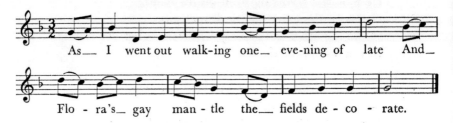

As— I went out walk-ing one— eve-ning of late And—
Flo - ra's— gay man - tle the— fields de - co - rate.

As I went out walking one evening of late
And Flora's gay mantle the fields decorate,

I carelessly wandered where I did know
On the banks of a fountain that flows in Glencoe.

With ribbons and tartans all around him did flow,
That fairest young Macdonald, the pride of Glencoe.

She seemed to enchant me, to her I drew nigh,
The red rose and lily on her cheeks seemed to vie.

I asked her her name and how far she did go.
Young man, she made answer, I'm going to Glencoe.

I said: My pretty fair maid, your enchantment is vile,[1]
Your beautiful features does my heart beguile.

And if your affection on me you'll bestow,
We'll bless the happy hour we met in Glencoe.

Young man, she made answer, your suit I disdain,
I once had a sweetheart, Macdonald by name.

He went to the wars about ten years ago,
And a maid I'll remain till he returns to Glencoe.

Perhaps young Macdonald regards not your name,
But has placed his affections on some foreign dame.

Macdonald from his promise will never depart,
But it's love, truth and honour I found in his heart.

[1] See Note on p. 283.

THE PRIDE OF GLENCOE

And if he is married still single I'll go
And I'll mourn for Macdonald, the pride of Glencoe.

When he saw she was loyal he pulled out a glove
That she gave him when parting as a token of love.

She lay on his breast while the tears did flow,
Saying: Are you returned to my arms in Glencoe.

Fair maid, he made answer, your sorrows are o'er,
While life does remain we shall never part no more.

The dangers of war at a distance may blow,
But in peace and contentment we'll reside in Glencoe.

Sung by Mrs. W. J. (Bride) Curran (43) at Conception Harbour, 23rd
October 1929

THE BLIND BEGGAR'S DAUGHTER OF BETHNAL GREEN

A

It was of a blind beg-gar, long— time he's been blind, He is called the blind beg-gar from— Beth-le-hem Tyne, And his marks and his— to-kens un-to you— I— will tell; He's con-tin-ual-ly led— by a dog, chain and bell.

It was of a blind beggar, long time he's been blind,
He is called the blind beggar from Bethlehem Tyne,
And his marks and his tokens unto you I will tell;
He's continually led by a dog, chain and bell.

The first one to court her was a captain so bright,
He came to court Betsy, 'twas late in the night,
Saying: My ship that sails over I'll discern[1] unto thee
If you tell me your father, my bonny Betsy.

The next came to court her was a merchant so bright,
He came to court Betsy by day and by night,
Saying: My stores and my goods I'll discern unto thee
If you tell me your father, my bonny Betsy.

The next came to court her was a squire so bright,
He came to court Betsy by day and by night,
Saying: My gold and my silver I'll discern unto thee
If you tell me your father, my bonny Betsy.

[1] In other versions 'resign'.

THE BLIND BEGGAR'S DAUGHTER

My father is a beggar, long time he's been blind,
He's called the blind beggar from Bethlehem Tyne,
His marks and his token unto you I will tell;
He's continually led by a dog, chain and bell.

Then up speaks the captain: For her I'll not have.
Then up speaks the merchant: For her I'll not crave.
Then up speaks the squire: Let the beggar agree,
You have welcome to my heart, my bonny Betsy.

Her old agèd father he stood at the door;
Don't reflect on my daughter because she is poor,
Because she's not dressed in the richest apparel.
On her I'll draw spangles, my bonny brown girl.

Her old father drew spangles that reached to the ground,
And the squire he laid her down ten thousand pounds,
And when he had laid down the last of his store,
'Twas then the blind beggar lay down ten thousand times more.

Sung by Mrs. May McCabe at North River, Conception Bay, 17th October
1929

B

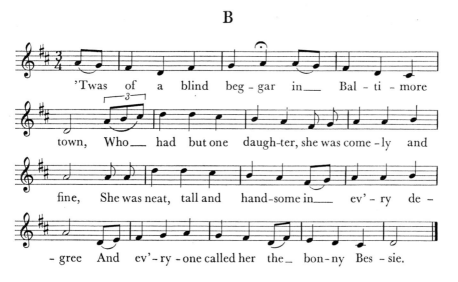

'Twas of a blind beg-gar in__ Bal-ti-more
town, Who__ had but one daugh-ter, she was come-ly and
fine, She was neat, tall and hand-some in__ ev'-ry de-
-gree And ev'-ry-one called her the_ bon-ny Bes-sie.

Sung by Mr. William Nosworthy at Clarke's Beach, Conception Bay, 14th
October 1929

189

THE RETURNED LOVER

C

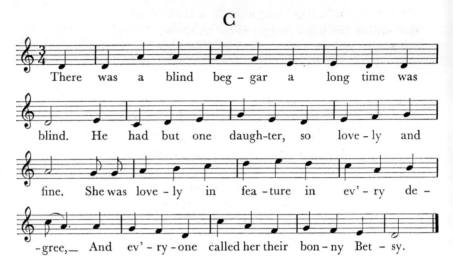

There was a blind beg – gar a long time was blind. He had but one daugh-ter, so love – ly and fine. She was love – ly in fea – ture in ev' – ry de – gree,— And ev' – ry – one called her their bon – ny Bet – sy.

Sung by Mr. James Walsh at Ferryland, 3rd August 1930

D

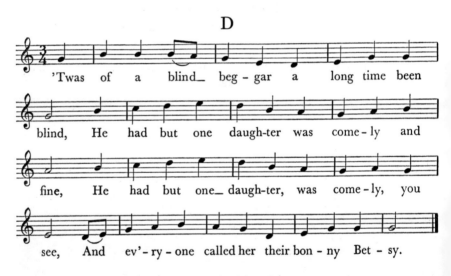

'Twas of a blind— beg – gar a long time been blind, He had but one daugh-ter was come – ly and fine, He had but one— daugh-ter, was come – ly, you see, And ev' – ry – one called her their bon – ny Bet – sy.

Sung by Mrs. Augustus James and Mrs. Margaret Mullins at Rencontre, Fortune Bay, 19th July 1930

Rejected and False-hearted Lovers

58 FLORO

A

As__ I rov - ed out__ one morn-ing in Spring, To
hear the lark whist - le and the night - in - gale sing, / O
green grow the__ rush - es all cov - ered with young, And__
small birds all____ round me, how joy - ful they sound.

As I roved out one morning in Spring,
To hear the lark whistle and the nightingale sing,
O green grows the rushes all covered with young,
And small birds all round me how joyful they sound.

Was there ever a young man so happy as me,
There is me and my Floro, my Floro and me,
I will go to young Floro and this I will say,
Saying: Let us get married, love, mention the day.

To wed a young shepherd, kind sir, I'm too young,
To wed a young shepherd, my time is not come;
I'll first be a servant until I am twenty-one
And then we will get married if love follows on.

To fulfil her promise in service she went,
To wait on a lady it was her intent,
To wait on a lady, a rich lady gay,
When young Floro was clothed in some costly array.

When eight months being over and nine coming on,
I wrote a letter to know her intent.
The answer she sent back to me: I'll lead a quite single life,
Before I will zeal [*sic*][1] to be a poor shepherd's wife.

[1] 'For I never intend to be' in another version.

REJECTED AND FALSE-HEARTED LOVERS

In reading those few lines it grieved my heart sore,
To think of lovely Floro that I'll ne'er see no more.
My heart is ensnared with her snowy-white breast;
I'm in love with young Floro and can't take no rest.

Farewell lonesome valley, I will now bid adieu,
Likewise to young Floro that proved so untrue,
Likewise to young Floro that proved so unkind,
Here's adieu to a false lover that soon changed her mind.

Sung by Mrs. Bridget Hall at North River, Conception Bay, 16th October
1929

B

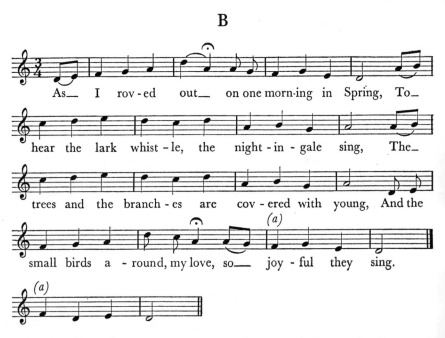

Sung by Mr. Fred Mercer at Upper Island Cove, Conception Bay, 10th
October 1929

FLORO

C

Sung by Mrs. G. H. Snow at North River, Conception Bay, 19th October
1929

59 A MAN IN LOVE

A

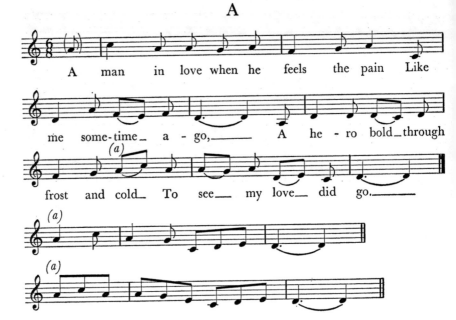

A man in love when he feels the pain Like
me some-time_ a - go,_____ A he - ro bold_through
frost and cold_ To see__ my love__ did go._____

A man in love when he feels the pain
Like me some time ago,
A hero bold through frost and cold
To see my love did go.

The moon shone bright to show me light
Along my dreary way,
And when I came to my own love's house
I knocked at the door so low.

She got up and she let me in,
Most lively I did go.
With her step so light and her voice so sweet,
Her hair in ringlets did flow.
I stole one kiss from her ruby lips[1]
Where all of my fancy goes.[1]

Will you go to your room, I said.
Or will you go to your bed,
Or will you go to some lonely grove?
In the morning we'll both be wed.

[1] Repeat the third and fourth phrases of the tune.

A MAN IN LOVE

I will not go to my room, she said,
Young man, you'll never prove true.
I'll sit you down by the clear fireside,
In the morning I'll talk to you.

Seven long years I courted you
Against your parents will,
Always intending to marry you,
But now, my love, farewell.

My ship lies off in the harbour,
She's bound to Columby's shore,
So I bid adieu to my true love,
Here's adieu for evermore.

Sung by Mr. John Hunt at Dunville, Placentia, 8th July 1930

B

The moon that light-ed me o - ver the plain, My
true— love for to go see,— I was of-ten-times tossed by the
win - try winds, And wet by the morn - ing dew.—

Sung by Mrs. Susan Dusey at Marystown, Placentia Bay, 11th July 1930

195

REJECTED AND FALSE-HEARTED LOVERS

C

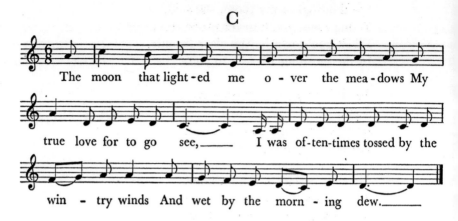

The moon that light-ed me o - ver the mea-dows My true love for to go see,_____ I was of-ten-times tossed by the win - try winds And wet by the morn - ing dew._____

Sung by Mrs. Mary Joseph Mitchell at Marystown, Placentia Bay, 12th July 1930

60 PROUD NANCY

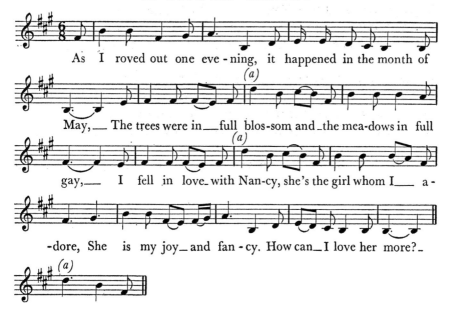

As I roved out one eve-ning, it happened in the month of
(a)
May,— The trees were in—full blos-som and—the mea-dows in full
(a)
gay,— I fell in love—with Nan-cy, she's the girl whom I— a-
-dore, She is my joy—and fan-cy. How can—I love her more?—
(a)

As I roved out one evening, it happened in the month of May,
The trees were in full blossom and the meadows in full gay,
I fell in love with Nancy, she's the girl whom I adore,
She is my joy and fancy. How can I love her more?

O Nancy, my love Nancy, O won't you marry me?
I've got no stores of riches, but I've got love for thee.
There's richer men than what I am, but none could love you so,
If I had gold as mountains it would be yours also.

To marry you in the bloom of youth, 'tis a thing I cannot do,
But since I've got your own consent, sure I can dance or sing,
I'm fitted for some richer gent, so I pray you now be gone.
Riches will suit me better; love will soon decline.

O Nancy, my love Nancy, it's now I'll take my leave;
Nor will I mourn for Nancy, she's a girl that will not grieve.
I'm here quite broken-hearted, it's plain for to be seen,
But will I mourn for Nancy, or wear the willow green?

The space of six months after this fair one changed her mind
She wrote me a loving letter hoping I would prove kind,
Saying: What I have said I'm sorry for, so I pray you now forgive,
And grant to me your fond favour in heart and hand to live.

197

REJECTED AND FALSE-HEARTED LOVERS

I wrote her back an answer all in a most scornful way,
Saying: Nancy, O love Nancy, don't think no more of me,
For I've another more suitable just taken of your place,
I'll let you know I can dance or sing if I never see your face.

Come all you pretty fair maids, a warning take by me,
Don't never spite your first true love for the sake of his poverty;
For riches they will wither away and your beauty will decay,
And for the object of your first true love you'll surely curse the day.

Sung by Mr. Robert Morgan at Blow-me-down, Conception Bay, 14th
October 1929

61 THE BLEACHES SO GREEN

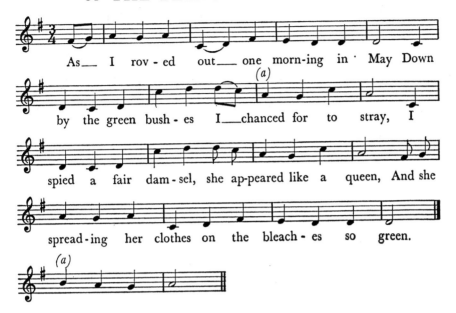

As I roved out one morning in May
Down by the green bushes I chanced for to stray,
I spied a fair damsel, she appeared like a queen,
And she spreading her clothes on the bleaches so green.

I drew up near her and this I did say:
You are the first that ever I have seen;
It's three years or better since it ran in my mind
That we would get married if you were inclined.

To get married, to get married, I think I'm too young,
Besides all you young men have a false flattering tongue.
My dad and mamma would be angry with me,
If I'd marry a rover, a rover like thee.

This young man stood up and he then walked away,
Saying: You may get better wherever they may be.
The sky it looks cloudy, I think it will rain.
They shook hands and they parted on the bleaches so green.

Come back, bonny laddie, and say you'll be mine,
Those last words you have spoke they have altered my mind.
If you've altered your mind, love, it's now all in vain;
I'll be courting some other on the bleaches so green.

REJECTED AND FALSE-HEARTED LOVERS

Some marry for riches, it's proud hearty way;
More marry for beauty, it's a flower will decay;
But if ever I get married it's bound to be seen,
The girl that proves true is the girl that wants me.

Sung by Mr. Joe Swayle Ewart at Trepassey, 3rd August 1930

62 THE SAUCY SAILOR

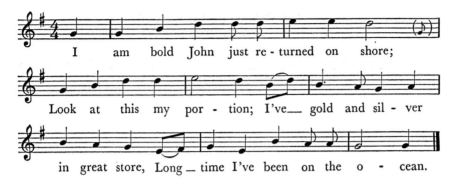

I am bold John just returned on shore;
Look at this my portion;
I've gold and silver in great store,
Long time I've been on the ocean.

I'll go up to my sweetheart's house
And see if she will have me or no,
Saying: Nancy, will you wed, Yes or No,
Wed with the tarry sailor?

O Nancy she turned around with a frown.
Do you think I'd marry you, no not I.
I want a man of high renown.
Do you think I would wed with a sailor?

O John put his hand into his purse,
Taking out two handfuls of gold,
Saying: Nancy, will you wed, Yes or No,
Wed with the tarry sailor?

O Nancy she turned around with a smile;
The sight of the money did her heart beguile.
I was only joking all the time;
To be sure I'll have my sailor.

If you were joking, I were in jest
It's only the cash to you I . . .
So I see 'tis the money you love best,
So you will never get your sailor.

REJECTED AND FALSE-HEARTED LOVERS

O John sat up in public mine [*sic*]
Plenty of gold and silver kind,[1]
Which made poor Nancy fret and frown
For the day she refused her sailor.

Sung by Mr. Richard Adams (80) at Milton, near Shoal Harbour, 29th
September 1929

[1] See Note, on p. 284.

63 EARLY, EARLY IN THE SPRING

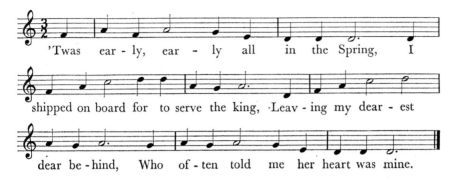

'Twas ear-ly, ear-ly all in the Spring, I shipped on board for to serve the king, ·Leav-ing my dear-est dear be-hind, Who of-ten told me her heart was mine.

'Twas early, early all in the Spring,
I shipped on board for to serve the king,
Leaving my dearest dear behind,
Who often told me her heart was mine.

I took her into my folding arms,
I taught her body a thousand charms,
With lamenting tears and kisses sweet,
Saying: We'll be married the next time we meet.

I was not long sailing over the deep
When an opportunity I chanced to meet;
I wrote a letter unto my dear,
But not one word from her could I hear.

When I came to her father's hall,
For my dearest dear I did call.
Her agèd father made thus reply:
Your dearest dear have left you and I.

I asked her father what did he mean.
He said my dearest is married to a Dane,
To a richer man than you for life,
So you may go look for another wife.

My curse on gold and bright silver too,
And all false lovers don't prove true.
I'll sail the ocean until I die
And split the waves rolling mountains high.

203

REJECTED AND FALSE-HEARTED LOVERS

Since I did not gain her gallant crown
I'll sail the ocean right round and round,
I'll sail the ocean until I die,
And split the waves rolling mountains high.

Sung by Mrs. Thomas J. Lee at Riverhead, St. Mary's, 27th July 1930

64 THE STREAMS OF LOVELY NANCY
OR
THE DREAMS OF LOVELY NANCY
A

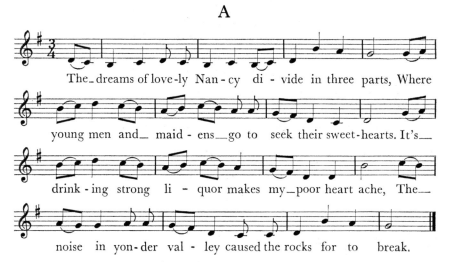

The_ dreams of love-ly Nan-cy di - vide in three parts, Where young men and_ maid - ens__go to seek their sweet-hearts. It's__ drink - ing strong li - quor makes my__poor heart ache, The__ noise in yon-der val - ley caused the rocks for to break.

The dreams of lovely Nancy divide in three parts,
Where young men and maidens go to seek their sweethearts.
It's drinking strong liquor makes my poor heart ache,
The noise in yonder valley caused the rocks for to break.

As a sailor and his true love was walking along,
Said the sailor to his true love: I will sing you a song.
It's a false-hearted woman caused me for to say,
Fare you well, lovely Nancy, I am bound away.

I'll go to some nunnery and it's there I'll spend my time,
I'll never get married and I'll be no man's bride,
I will never get married, no man's bride will I be
Until my own dearest Jimmy will return home to me.

I will go to yonder mountain where the wild fowl do fly;
There is one bird among them she fly very high.
If I had her in my arms one moment to stand,
You would see how I'd tame her by the sleight of my hand.

I will go to my captain and I will fall on my knees,
I will ask him a question if he may grant it to me.

REJECTED AND FALSE-HEARTED LOVERS

But the answer he made me: You may go back again,
Since your love is so little [fickle?] and that I know well.

I will go to my castle where the castle do stand,
It's built up with ivory all on the dark strand,
It's built up with ivory and diamonds so bright,
It's a signal for sailors on a dark stormy night.

The bright star of old Erion so beautiful do shine,
With her hair over her shoulder like amber brown;
She delights in my company more than gold I declare;
Although she do slight me she's the girl I love dear.

Sung by Mrs. James Joe Doyle at Gooseberry Cove, Cape Shore, Placentia
Bay, 7th July 1930

B

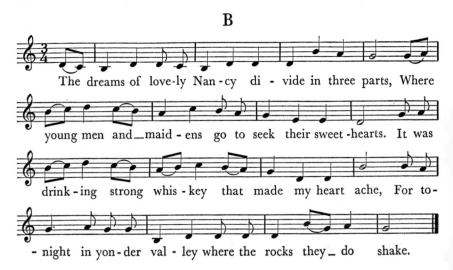

The dreams of love-ly Nan-cy di-vide in three parts, Where young men and—maid-ens go to seek their sweet-hearts. It was drink-ing strong whis-key that made my heart ache, For to-night in yon-der val-ley where the rocks they— do shake.

The dreams of lovely Nancy divide in three parts,
Where young men and maidens go to seek their sweethearts.
It was drinking strong whiskey that made my heart ache,
For tonight in yonder valley where the rocks they do shake.

It's a sailor and his true love were walking along;
Said the sailor to his true love: I will sing you a song.
It's a false-hearted woman causes me for to say:
Fare you well, lovely Nancy, I'm now bound away.

I will go to some nunnery, I will there spend my life,
I'll never get married, I'll be no man's wife,

THE STREAMS OF LOVELY NANCY

I'll never get married, no man's wife I will be,
Then my dearest Nancy will return unto me.

I will go to yonder mountain where the wild fowl do fly,
There's one there among them she flies very high.
If I had her in my arms just one moment to spend,
She would see how I'd tame her by the sleight of my hand.

I will go to my father's castle, where the castle do stand,
It is built up with ivory all on the dark strand,
It is built up with ivory and diamonds so bright,
It's a signal for sailors on a dark stormy night.

The bright star of Erion so pleasant may shine,
With her hair over her shoulder of a deep, deepish brown.
I delight in her company more than gold I declare,
Although she did slight me, she's the one I love dear.

Sung by Mrs. Maurice Flinn at Placentia, 6th July 1930

65 DOWN BY A RIVERSIDE

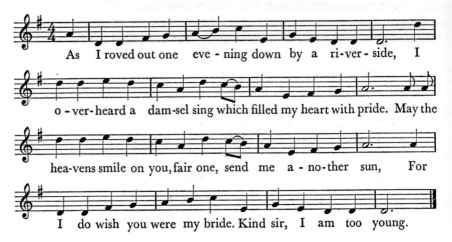

As I roved out one evening down by a riverside,
I overheard a damsel sing which filled my heart with pride.
May the heavens smile on you, fair one, send me another sun[?],
For I do wish you were my bride. Kind sir, I am too young.

The younger you are, my pretty fair maid, the better you are for me,
For I readily swear and do declare my lovely bride you will be.
He took her by the lily-white hand, he kissed her cheeks and chin,
And he took her to his own bedroom to spend the night with him.

O the first part of the night they frolicked and they played,
And the next part of the night close in his arms she lay.
The night being spent and the day coming on and the morning sun
                                                              appeared,
This young man arose, put on his clothes, saying: Fare you well, my
                                                              dear.

O that's not the promise you made to me down by a riverside,
You promised that you'd marry me, make me your loving bride.
If I promised that I'd marry you, it's more than I can do,
For I never intend to marry a girl so easily led as you.

You go down your father's garden and there you'll cry your fill,
And when you think on what you've done you can blame your own
                                                              free will.
There is a rose in your father's garden, some people call it rue,
When fish will fly and seas run dry, young men they will prove true.

DOWN BY A RIVERSIDE

There's lots of girls go to the fair which I've been often before,
But me, poor thing, must stay at home rocking the cradle o'er,
Rocking the cradle o'er and o'er, singing sweet lullaby.
Was there ever a girl in this wide world so easily led as I?

Sung by Mrs. Violet McCabe at North River, Conception Bay, 19th October
1929

Hard-hearted Parents

66 THE FATHER IN AMBUSH

There's a tree— in my fa-ther's gar-den, love-ly Jim-my, said she, Where young men and— maid-ens do— meet— of— thee, Where young men and— maid-ens do— take their si-lent rest, Meet— with their love-ly Jim-my, you're the boy I love best.

There's a tree in my father's garden, lovely Jimmy, said she,
Where young men and maidens do meet of thee,
Where young men and maidens do take their silent rest,
Meet with their lovely Jimmy, you're the boy I love best.

O last Saturday evening near the concerning wall [*sic*]
Where I spied lovely Jimmy, straight, handsome and tall,
She said: Will you come to me a piece down the road
For to view my father's dwelling, it's a place of repose.

Now her father in ambush, in ambush he lay,
A-listening to all that his daughter did say.
O daughter, dear daughter, I will avenge you,
And 'tis with a long weapon he pierced my love through.

Now then father, cruel father and that was your plan,
The innocent blood of my Jimmy you've slain.
I'll heave myself down in the ground where he lies.
May the heavens shine round him, he's my own darling boy.

O come dig my love a grave both long, wide and deep,
And I'll plant round him the lily so sweet.

THE FATHER IN AMBUSH

I'll heave myself down on the ground where he lies.
May the heavens shine round him, he's my own darling boy.

O then green grows the rushes and the tops of them small,
For love it's a killing pain hangs over us all,
For love it's a killing pain like a sword pierced my breast,
And the grave it's the next place I'm in hopes to find rest.

Sung by Mr. Michael Corbett at Lake View, Harbour Main, Conception
Bay, 25th October 1929

67 JOHNNY DOYLE

Now 'twas of a—— fair—maid was wan-der-ing in love And
mak-ing of her moan— to the great God a-bove, And
mak-ing of her moan,—say-ing: I think it's high time To be
rolled in the arms— of my own— John-ny Doyle.

(a)

Now 'twas of a fair maid was wandering in love
And making of her moan to the great God above,
And making of her moan, saying: I think it's high time
To be rolled in the arms of my own Johnny Doyle.

It was on a Sunday evening we made up this plan
And 'twas early Monday morning 'twas to be carried out.
Where the servant maid was listening to all we did say;
She went straight to my mamma and gave me away.

She locked me in a corner [tower?] so lonely and so high,
Where no one could pity me or hear my sad cry.
She sent for Willie Coborn to come to marry me,
A man that I hated and didn't want to see.

The horses they got ready and the carriages likewise;
We drove along together till we came to Claudy town.
Where they drove with pleasure and I drove with toil.
I leave my heart behind me with young Johnny Doyle.

Where the gates they stand open and the clergy they walked out;
To him I gave my heart away with a great deal of toil,
Saying: I'd far sooner marry my own Johnny Doyle.

Now we will send for Johnny Doyle, my dear, before it is too late.

JOHNNY DOYLE

You can send for Johnny Doyle, mamma, but now it is too late.
For the distance is so far and my pains they are so great.

Now the horses they got ready with my father I drove home,
Saying: Mamma, dearest mamma, take me to my room.
Willie Coborn will never enjoy me or call me his wife,
For I pray this very night to put an end to my life.

'Twas early the next morning this fair woman was found dead,
With Johnny Doyle's silk handkerchief all tied round her head.
And when she was dying said: Johnny dear, farewell.
There's more between you and me than any tongue can tell.

The day of Mary's funeral it was a glorious sight
To see four and twenty fair maids all dressed in white.
They took her to St. Mary's church and laid her in the soil,
Saying: There lies the darling of young Johnny Doyle.

Sung by Mr. James Heaney at Stock Cove, Bonavista Bay, 20th September
1929

68 THERE WAS A LADY IN THE EAST

There was a la - dy in the East, Her age it was scarce twen - ty. She had sweet - hearts of the best, Both lords and squi - res plen - ty. She had sweet - hearts of the best, But real - ly those up - on her, But she a-dored her fa-ther's clerk More than a man of hon - our.

There was a lady in the East,
Her age it was scarce twenty.
She had sweethearts of the best,
Both lords and squires plenty.
She had sweethearts of the best,
But really those upon her [sic],
But she adored her father's clerk
More than a man of honour.

As she was walking the hall one day
Her father chanced to meet her.
Are you going to throw yourself away,
You silly fond young creature?
Are you going to marry a servant man
Without either birth or breeding?
Not one pound portion will you gain
While this is my intention.

Down on her bended knees she fell,
Saying: Father, use your pleasure,
For I adore my Jimmy dear
More than your earthly treasure.
I still adore my Jimmy dear,
With him I am intended
And if kind providence suffers me
With him I am intended.

THERE WAS A LADY IN THE EAST

There was a table in the hall,
A loaded pistol on it.
'Twas to her small lily-white breast
She quickly did discharge it.
It was to her small lily-white breast
As she knelt down before it.
The very last words she ever said:
I will and shall adore him.

When her father came to see
The crime he had committed,
He wrung his hands and tore his hair
Just like a one distracted.
When her mother came to see
The corpse lie there a-bleeding,
A fainting fit came on so quick
Which caused the mother's ruin.

Fair young Jimmy among them all
With his lily-white hands a-wringing,
He kissed the blue veins of her breast
Just as the blood rolled spilling,
Saying: Why did you treat my darling so,
Or why were you so cruel?
Why didn't you lay the blame on me
And spare to me my jewel?

He took a small knife in his hand,
Saying: Here I'll stay no longer.
He cuts the slender threads of life.
Alone with my love I'll wander.

They both were buried in one grave
As two true lovers loyal.
May the heavens above protect such loves
And send them no such trials.

Out of his grave there grew a branch
And out of hers a briar,
Which grew together in a true love's knot
Which caused far and near to admire.

Sung by Mr. John Donovan at Broad Cove, Bonavista Bay, 23rd September
1929

69 THE BONNY LABOURING BOY

As I roved out one evening all in the blooming Spring,
I spied a lovely fair maid who grievously did sing,
Saying: Cruel was my parents who did me so deny
And would not let me marry my bonny labouring boy.

Young Johnnie was my true love's name as you can plainly see;
My father he employed him his labouring boy to be,
To harrow, reap and sow the seed and plough my father's land
And soon I fell in love with him as you may understand.

I courted him for twelve long months but little did I know
That my cruel parents would prove my overthrow.
They watched us close one evening while in a shady grove,
Pledging our vows together in constant bands of love.

My father he stepped up to me and seized me by the hand
And swore he'd send young Johnnie into some foreign land.
He locked me in my bedroom my comfort to deny
And left me there to grieve and mourn for my bonny labouring boy.

My mother came next morning and thus to me did say:
Your father has intended to appoint your wedding-day.
I nobly made answer: With him I'll ne'er comply,
But single will I still remain for my bonny labouring boy.

Said the daughter to the mother: Your plans are all in vain,
Your lords and dukes and earls, their riches I disdain.

THE BONNY LABOURING BOY

I'd rather live a single life my time I will employ
Increasing nature's prospects for my bonny labouring boy.

So fill your glasses to the brim; the toast goes merrily round.
Here's a health to every labouring boy that ploughs and sows the
ground.
And when his work is over to his home he'll go with joy,
And happy is the girl that gets her bonny labouring boy.

Sung by Mrs. Lucy Heaney at Stock Cove, Bonavista Bay, 22nd September
1929

70 ON BOARD THE GALLEE

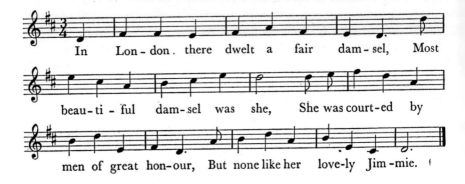

In Lon - don. there dwelt a fair dam - sel, Most
beau - ti - ful dam - sel was she, She was court - ed by
men of great hon - our, But none like her love - ly Jim - mie.

In London there dwelt a fair damsel,
Most beautiful damsel was she,
She was courted by men of great honour,
But none like her lovely Jimmie.

When her father he first came to hear it,
And an angry old man was he,
Saying: Daughter, I'm told you're engaged
To a man that's below your degree.

Don't believe no such stories, dear father,
Don't believe no such stories on me,
For if ever I am inclined to get married,
It will be a man that's above my degree.

Her father he flew in a passion,
Like a man quite distracted did run.
It was into her room quite conveniently,
And brought out a well-lovèd gun.

Two choices, two choices, dear daughter,
Two choices I'll give unto thee,
Saying: Which would you rather I'd shoot him
Or send him on board the Gallee.

I thank you, dear honourable father,
For those choices you gave unto me;
I would rather see Jimmie a-sailing
Than his innocent blood spilled for me.

218

ON BOARD THE GALLEE

My father he wants me to marry
A man that is very old,
But I would not lie in his bed, Jimmie,
No, not for a fortune of gold.

But Jimmie and I will be married,
And our friends all invited will be;
There'll be young men to wait upon Jimmie
And fair maids to wait upon me.

Sung by Mr. J. T. Fitzpatrick at Marystown, Placentia Bay, 13th July 1930

71 YOUNG M'TYRE

There was a man lived in the East, He had one on-ly daugh-ter, And she fell a - court-ing with young M'- - Tyre, Who was ser-vant to her fa-ther.

There was a man lived in the East,
He had one only daughter,
And she fell a-courting with young M'Tyre,
Who was servant to her father.

She heard her father swear one day
It's him he's put the hoax on,
It's young M'Tyre I will transport
For my daughter lies in danger.

She arose, put on her clothes
And holloaed loud to wake him.
Arise, M'Tyre, and go your way
For you know who lies in danger.

How can I go and leave this place?
I'm a poor distressèd stranger.
How can I go and leave this place
And go without my wages?

Here's a hundred guineas all in bright gold,
It's more than my father owes you.
Take this, M'Tyre, and go your way,
For you know I do adore you.

She laid her head upon his shoulder
About one half an hour;
Kind loving words were then they spoke
While the tears from her eyes did pour.

YOUNG M'TYRE

. . . .
They kissed, shook hands and parted.
He's gone, he's gone, this fair one cries,
And has left me broken-hearted.

Then the lords came to court this fair one,
They came to court Miss Nancy.
But none of them would ever she wed,
There was none to please her fancy.

Her father asked her the reason why,
To him she told her fancy.
No man on earth will ever I wed
Since you banished young M'Tyre.

He says: My dear, I did not know
How dearly did you love him,
And you can go and fetch him back
Since there's none on earth you love above him.

She wrote a letter all in great haste,
She sent it to M'Tyre;
She fetched him back that very same day,
Made a lord of young M'Tyre.

Sung by Mrs. Joseph McCarthy at St. Jacques, Fortune Bay, 17th July 1930

221

72 THE RICH MERCHANT'S DAUGHTER

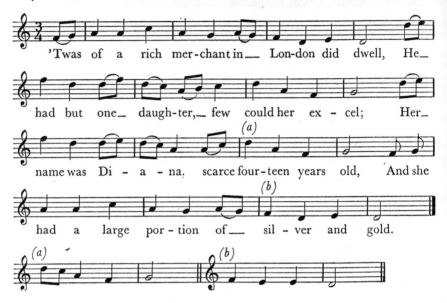

'Twas of a rich merchant in London did dwell,
He had but one daughter, few could her excel;
Her name was Diana, scarce fourteen years old,
And she had a large portion of silver and gold.

It happened to be on a fine summer's day,
When the ship of her father sailed into the quay.
Among other fair maids on board she did go
For to view her father's ship and his lovely cargo.

She had not been there but a short space of time
When on a young sailor she placèd her mind.
She got into a boat and rowed quickly to the shore
And was seized by a pain that she never felt before.

O where's my maid Betsy, come bring her to me,
To see if she'll relieve me one moment or three.
The torment of love is more than I can bear,
And if she can't relieve me, I'm ruined, I fear.

O Betsy, lovely Betsy, come hasten to my dear
And tell him there's somebody waiting for him here.

THE RICH MERCHANT'S DAUGHTER

In a short time after, she asked was he come.
And he quickly made answer: Yes, madam, I am.

Now don't you remember upon a certain day
When a ship of my father sailed into the quay,
That day I lost a jewel more precious than gold,
And you are the young man that found it I am told.

O the sailor he blushed like a man in despair;
The more he did blush, the more on him did stare,
Saying: My heart was the jewel you stole away from me,
So grant me your love or else ruined I'll be.

Now this couple got married I heard people say,
Great nobles attended on their wedding day.
They're living together and parents also
Since providence proved kind to me to the seas I'll no more go.

Sung by Mr. George Dover at Beaubois, Placentia Bay, 11th July 1930

73 BOUND DOWN TO DERRY

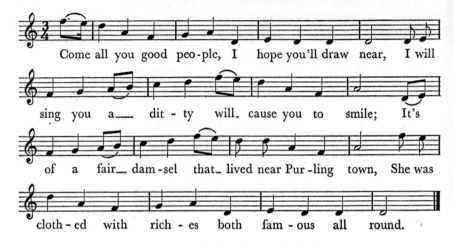

Come all you good peo-ple, I hope you'll draw near, I will
sing you a— dit - ty will. cause you to smile; It's
of a fair— dam-sel that— lived near Pur-ling town, She was
cloth - ed with rich - es both fam - ous all round.

Come all you good people, I hope you'll draw near,
I will sing you a ditty will cause you to smile;
It's of a fair damsel that lived near Purling town,
She was clothèd with riches, both famous all round.

As she was a-walking and her dress was milk-white,
And all that stood by her was shocked with delight.
They was lords, dukes and squires, but they all proved in vain;
There was not one of them could that fair lady gain.

Herself and her father was walking one day;
A brisk young sailor by chance came that way.
He was jolly, brisk and merry as he passed her by,
And she kindly saluted him and bid him draw nigh.

She says: My young man, come tell me your name,
Come tell me your land, come tell me the same.
I am bound down to Derry, young lady, says he,
And James was the name my godfather gave me.

Now, James, in this country I would have you to bide,
And your wedding-day I will be your fond bride.
It's put gold in your pocket and my life I'll lay down
That you are the first young man that sailed the world around.

O no then, fair lady, O no then, said he;
There's parts of this wide world that I never see.

BOUND DOWN TO DERRY

What would your old agèd father then say
To marry a sailor was storing away?
I am bound down to Derry, a place I abode
And I hope there's no danger in travelling this road.

Up speaks her old father that stood there in sight,
You can have my pretty daughter to be your fond bride.
I'll put gold in your pocket and silver in store,
And James, I'll advise you to ramble no more.

It's early next morning to church they did go,
On a fine summer morning they called a great show.
They was lords, dukes and squires was there to be seen
To see lovely Jimmy and his beautiful queen.

Sung by Mr. Michael (FitzGibbons) Corbett (60) at Lake View, Harbour
Main, Conception Bay, 25th October 1929

74 KIND FORTUNE

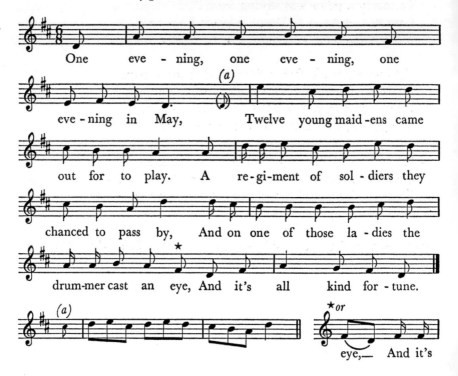

One evening, one evening, one evening in May,
Twelve young maidens came out for to play.
A regiment of soldiers they chanced to pass by,
And on one of those ladies the drummer cast an eye,
And it's all kind fortune.

Said this little drummer to his com-er-ades,
Saying: One of those ladies my heart she has won, [*bis*]
And if she denies me I'm surely undone,
And it's all hard fortune.

Early next morning the drummer arose
And dressed himself out in his best suit of clothes,
With his watch in his fob and his sword in his hand,
And he went to the lady right down to the strand,
And it's all kind fortune.

He took off his hat and he made a low bow,
Saying: Miss, I ask pardon for making so free.
Dear honourable lady, my heart you have won,

KIND FORTUNE

And if you deny me I'm surely undone,
'Twill be all hard fortune.

You silly little drummer, O what do you mean?
My father is a captain of honour and fame,
And I am his daughter dearest to thee [him].
Would you think would I bind myself down to slav'ry?
'Twould be all kind fortune.

My soul shall go quickly to heaven or hell,
For my innocent blood I will spill.
'Tis with my broadsword I'll strike
And I'll cut down the innocent threads of my life,
'Twill be all hard fortune.

O come back, little drummer, I'm here at your will;
'Tis pity your innocent blood for to spill.
We'll saddle our horse and to Plymouth we will go
And it's there we will get married in spite of our foe,
And it's all kind fortune.

And when we are married and all past and been,
What can they say but we followed the drum,
And it's all kind fortune.

Sung by Mr. Michael Carrol at Placentia, 7th July 1930

A

In— Bris-tol lived a dam-sel, Her age was scarce six-teen, And court-ed she was by— ma - ny Her fa -vour for to win.

In Bristol lived a damsel,
Her age was scarce sixteen,
And courted she was by many
Her favour for to win.

Till at length up stepped a drummer
And gave to her one kiss,
And said: Dear honoured lady,
In the regiment will you 'list?

O yes, replied the damsel,
And that I'll surely do,
For I do like your music
And likewise your rat-tat-too.

O then, replied the drummer,
. . . .
Then I'm afraid that you won't wed,
With a poor young man like me.

O that you may depend on,
The lady made reply,
For if I don't wed with you, young man,
I will never be made a bride.

This couple they got married,
And servants at their call,
And now he's knocked off playing
Among his comrades all.

Sung by Mr. William Ball at Hermitage, 21st July 1930

THE DISCHARGED DRUMMER

B

In Bristol lived a lady, Her age it was sixteen, Court-ed she was by many And her fa-vour for to win.

In Bristol lived a lady,
Her age it was sixteen,
Courted she was by many
And her favour for to win.

But none of them could suit her,
Nor please her to her mind,
Till at last there came a drummer,
So willing and so kind.

Where the drummer stepped up to her
And he stole from her one kiss,
And he said: Dear honoured lady,
In the regiment will you 'list?

And if you will consent for to marry
Or to lie by my side,
I will buy you your discharge, my love,
In a carriage you will ride.

O yes, replied the drummer,
How happy should I be,
But I'm afraid that you won't lie
With a such young man as me.

O yes, replied the lady,
And this I'll surely do,
For while I love your music sweet,
Likewise your rat-tat-too.

Sung by Mr. George Taylor at Grole, Hermitage Bay, 23rd July 1930

76 GREEN BROOM

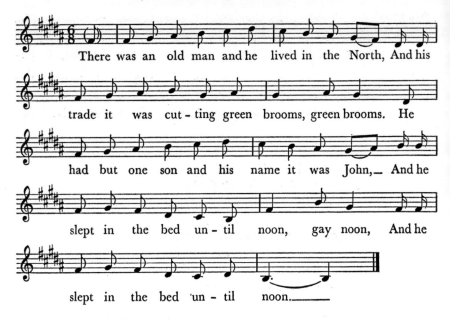

There was an old man and he lived in the North, And his
trade it was cut-ting green brooms, green brooms. He
had but one son and his name it was John,— And he
slept in the bed un-til noon, gay noon, And he
slept in the bed 'un-til noon.————

There was an old man and he lived in the North,
And his trade it was cutting green brooms, green brooms.
He had but one son and his name it was John,
And he slept in the bed until noon, gay noon,
And he slept in the bed until noon.

The old man arose and he put on his clothes.
He swore he'd set fire to John's room, gay room,
If he would not rise and sharpen his knives
To go in the woods to cut broom, green broom,
To go in the woods to cut broom.

John went away and not one word did say
Till he came to a castle of fame, great fame,
He knocked at the gate with courage so great.
Fair maid, will you buy any broom, green broom,
Fair maid will you buy any broom?

Out came the maid and this she did say:
My mistress wants you in her room, gay room.
From you she would like, from you she will buy
One dozen or two of your brooms, green brooms,
One dozen or two of your brooms.

GREEN BROOM

And gents or ladies, say what you will,
He got her by cutting of broom, green broom,
He got her by cutting of broom.

Sung by Mrs. Sarah Mercer at Upper Island Cove, Conception Bay, 11th
October 1929

A

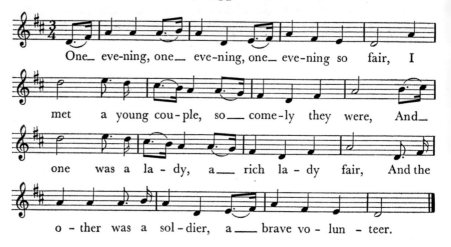

One evening, one evening, one evening so fair,
I met a young couple, so comely they were,
And one was a lady, a rich lady fair,
And the other was a soldier, a brave volunteer.

They had not been walking past one mile or two,
When out of his knapsack a fiddle he drew;
He made such music on the tip of the string
On the banks of the river where the nightingales sing.

The soldier to the lady: 'Tis time to go home.
O no, cried the lady, we'll have one more tune.
Your tune it entices me one tip of the string,
On the banks of the river where the nightingales sing.

The lady to the soldier: Will you marry me?
O no, cried the soldier, that never shall be;
I've a wife in old Ireland and children have three
And another in Oporto is too many for me.

I will go back to old Ireland, I'll stay there one year,
And instead of cold water I'll drink whisky clear,
And if ever I return it shall be in the Spring
To watch the water gliding and hear the nightingales sing.

THE NIGHTINGALE

Come all you pretty maidens wheresoever you be,
And never court a soldier of any degree;
They'll kiss you and court you and leave you behind
On the banks of the river to hear the nightingales sing.

Sung by Mr. John Parsons at Hermitage, 21st July 1930

B

Sung by Miss Florrie Snow at North River, Conception Bay, 18th October
1929

78 SOLDIER, WILL YOU MARRY ME

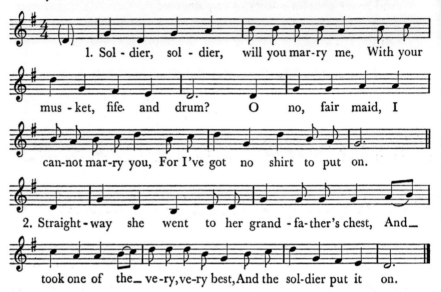

1. Sol - dier, sol - dier, will you mar-ry me, With your mus - ket, fife and drum? O no, fair maid, I can-not mar-ry you, For I've got no shirt to put on.

2. Straight - way she went to her grand - fa-ther's chest, And took one of the ve-ry, ve-ry best, And the sol-dier put it on.

Soldier, soldier, will you marry me,
With your musket, fife and drum?
O no, fair maid, I cannot marry you,
For I've got no shirt to put on.
Straightway she went to her grandfather's chest,
And took one of the very, very best,
And the soldier put it on.

In subsequent stanzas the following articles are substituted for 'shirt', and where necessary 'a pair' is substituted for 'one'.

Pants	Vest	Boots
Socks	Coat	Cap

Last stanza (sung to the tune of the first eight bars)

Soldier, soldier, will you marry me,
With your musket, fife and drum?
O no, fair maid, that's a thing that cannot be,
For I have a wife of my own.

Sung by Mrs. Violet McCabe at North River, Conception Bay, 19th October 1929

79 YOUNG MEN, COME MARRY ME

As I roved out one morning in the lovely month of May,
I met a pretty fair one, these words I heard her say:
O father, I'm sixteen years of age, I'm weary of my life,
O father, I think it's almost time for me to be made a wife.

O hold your tongue, dear daughter, O hold your tongue, said he,
For men they are deceitful and flattering tongues, he said.
O what cares I for flattering tongues, for flattering tongues, she said,
At the time you married my mamma, she wasn't so old as me.

I have a sister Mary and that you all [well?] do know.
She have not long been married, only nine long months ago.
She has a baby for herself to daddle upon her knee,
And I think it's time for me to have one, for I'm nearly as old as she.

Besides a good wife I would make, I would never on him frown;
I'd keep a shilling for to spend with any girls in town,
I'd keep a shilling for to spend and I'd never be afraid.
I pray, young men, come marry me, don't let me die a maid.

WOOING AND COURTSHIP

The bell-man he went round the town to see what he could find,
A soldier, or a sailor to please this fair one's mind,
A soldier, or a sailor, no matter who, said she.
For I would roll him in my arms and I'd use him tenderly.

Sung by Mr. Thomas Ghaney at Conception Harbour, 24th October 1929

80 THE NEW MOWN HAY

As I roved out one evening in the lovely month of May,
Down by a flowery garden I carelessly did stray,
Down by a flowery garden I carelessly did stray,
And there I spied a pretty young bride a-tossing out her hay.

Good morning, madam, I replied; good morning, sir, said she.
Have you the burden all alone to spread and toss your hay?
My brothers they are all gone to the bogs far away,
They left me here to bide alone to spread and toss my hay.

I'll be your humble servant, without any delay.
Whatever lies at your command I'm willing to obey,
Whatever lies at your command I'm willing to obey,
If you'll admit and give consent to spread and toss your hay.

I thank you for your offer, sir, so please pass on your way,
For if my papa comes to know it's angry he will be,
For if my papa comes to know it's angry he will be,
So go and leave me as you found me to spread and toss my hay.

WOOING AND COURTSHIP

I placed my arms around her waist and gently laid her down,
Upon her lips I placed a kiss which caused this girl to frown.
While she was in her merriment, sure I had time to play.
I cried, for shame, I played the game, I spoiled her new-mown hay.

You've spoiled my new mown hay, she cried, and something else
                                                            besides,
And bear the pride of honour you must make me your bride.
So call unto my father's house all at the break of day
And a noble fortune you will gain for tossing out my hay.

I called unto her father's house just at the break of day,
Ten thousand pounds he counted down all on my wedding day,
Ten thousand pounds he counted down all on my wedding day,
So, boys, don't I get damned well paid for tossing of her hay.

Sung by Mr. Dan Gash at Broad Cove, Bonavista Bay, 23rd September 1929

Love Laments and Lyrics

82 THE MAIDEN'S LAMENT

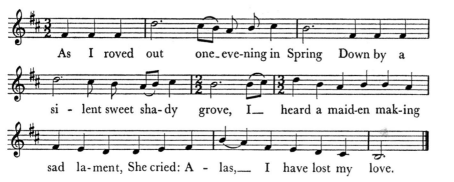

As I roved out one evening in Spring
Down by a silent sweet shady grove,
I heard a maiden making sad lament,
She cried: Alas, I have lost my love.

For he was always both loyal and constant,
And unto me his kind love did show,
Till my parents gave him the plain denial,
Love was the occasion of my overthrow.

Unkind parents, hard-hearted, cruel,
How could you owe me a great spite
To banish from me my own true lover
And in him place my whole heart's delight.

O was it because that he was an heiress,
Although his parents being poor and low;
If that be so then great is my mischance,
Love was the occasion of my overthrow.

Love is like an unquenching fire,
Like a raging fire it seems to burn.
Unto my cold grave I will retire,
Unto my friends I'll never return.

So farewell, father, and farewell, mother,
Farewell, friends, and farewell, foe,

LOVE LAMENTS AND LYRICS

Farewell, sisters, although to true lovers,
Love was the occasion of my overthrow.

Come all you fair maids like me a-dying,
It's now I'm taking my last farewell,
And all you small birds round me flying,
Let your sweet notes be my fasting [passing?] bell.

Sung by Mr. James Sullivan at King's Cove, Bonavista Bay, 28th September
1929

83 SHE'S LIKE THE SWALLOW

She's like the swal-low that flies so high, She's like the ri-ver that ne-ver runs dry, She's like the sun-shine on the lee shore. I love my love and love is no more.

She's like the swallow that flies so high,
She's like the river that never runs dry,
She's like the sunshine on the lee shore.
I love my love and love is no more.

'Twas out in the garden this fair maid did go,
Picking the beautiful prim-e-rose;
The more she plucked the more she pulled
Until she got her whole a-per-on full.

It's out of those roses she made a bed,
A stony pillow for her head.
Now this fair maid she lay down, no word did she say
Until this fair maid's heart was broke.

There are a man on yonder hill,
He got a heart as hard as stone.
He have two hearts instead of one.
How foolish must that girl be
For to think I love no other but she.

For the world was not meant for one alone,
The world was meant for every one.

Sung by Mr. John Hunt at Dunville, Placentia Bay, 8th July 1930

84 GREEN BUSHES

I'll buy you fine silks, I'll buy you fine gowns, I'll buy you pet-ti-coats that will flounce to the ground, If you'll spite your true love and will come to fol-low me, Bid a-dieu to the green bush-es and for e-ver will be.

Sung by Mr. James Walsh at Ferryland, 5th August 1930

85 THE CUCKOO

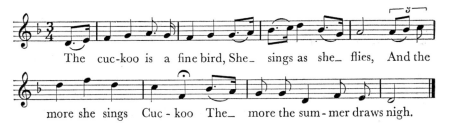

The cuc-koo is a fine bird, She_ sings as she_ flies, And the more she sings Cuc - koo The_ more the sum-mer draws nigh.

The cuckoo is a fine bird,
She sings as she flies,
And the more she sings Cuckoo
The more the summer draws nigh.

I wish I was a scholar
And could handle my pen,
I would write a private letter
To my true love I would send.

Sung by Mr. Joseph C. Jackman at Grole, Hermitage Bay, 23rd July 1930

86 THE MORNING DEW

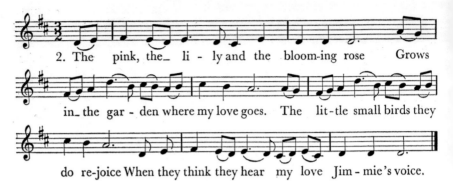

2. The pink, the_ li - ly and the bloom-ing rose Grows in_ the gar - den where my love goes. The lit-tle small birds they do re-joice When they think they hear my love Jim - mie's voice.

There's not one drop of morning dew
That's half as sweet as one kiss from you.

The pink, the lily and the blooming rose
Grows in the garden where my love goes.
The little small birds they do rejoice
When they think they hear my love Jimmie's voice.

Sung by Mrs. Sarah Mercer at Upper Island Cove, Conception Bay, 11th
October 1929

Nonsense Song

87 THE LIAR'S SONG

When I was a lit-tle ba - by, just a-ble to walk a -
(a)
- lone, I went to seek my for - tune, I tra-velled all a -
- lone. I put my foot on the strand shore and let my hand hang
down, I crossed all over the balm-y plain and ne-ver touched the ground.
(a)

When I was a little baby, just able to walk alone,
I went to seek my fortune, I travelled all alone.
I put my foot on the strand shore and let my hand hang down,
I crossed all over the balmy plain and never touched the ground.

I met a giant all on my way, so lofty and so high,
How earnestly he looked at me as I did pass him by;
I challenged him to sing or dance, to wrestle or to run,
And I bet him out of all his sport and I kicked him when I was done.

I built myself a little box about eighteen acres square,
I filled it up unto the brim with all bright silver clear.
I bought myself a coal-black dog as you might plainly see;
His legs were eighteen lanyards long and his paws were nine miles wide,
And around the world in half a day all on my dog did ride.[1]

I bought myself a flock of sheep, and all of them were wethers;
They sometimes bring me wool and more times bring me leather.
O was not that a very fine flock to bring such a great increase;
For every time the moon has changed they bring me six lambs apiece.

[1] Repeat the fourth line of the tune. See also Appendix, p. 335.

247

NONSENSE SONG

I bought myself a coal-black hen, as you might plainly see,
I sat her on some mussel-shells and she brought to me a mare,
And she brought to me a mare, my boys, so lofty and so high,
And any one will sing this song will surely sing a lie.

Sung by Mrs. Thomas J. Lee at Riverhead, St. Mary's, 27th July 1930

Cumulative Songs

88 THE TREE IN THE WOOD

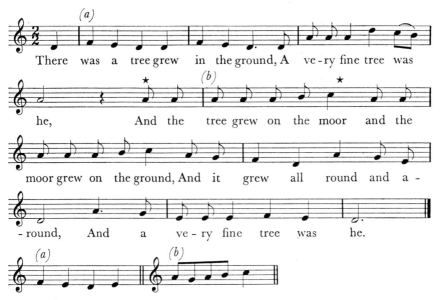

> There was a tree grew in the ground, A ve-ry fine tree was he, And the tree grew on the moor and the moor grew on the ground, And it grew all round and a-round, And a ve-ry fine tree was he.

★ The passage between asterisks is repeated as often as is required.

There was a tree grew in the ground,
A very fine tree was he,
And the tree grew on the moor,
And the moor grew on the ground,
And it grew all round and around,
And a very fine tree was he.

And on that tree there was a branch,
And a very fine branch was he,
And the branch was on the tree,
And the tree grew on the moor,
And the moor grew on the ground,
And it grew all round and around,
And a very fine tree was he.

Last stanza
And on that man there was a slip,
And a very fine slip was he,
And the slip was on the man,
And the man was on the bed,

And the bed was on the feather,
And the feather was on the down,
And the down was on the bird,
And the bird was in the egg,
And the egg was in the nest,
And the nest was on the branch,
And the branch was on the tree,
And the tree grew on the moor,
And the moor grew on the ground,
And it grew all round and around,
And a very fine tree was he.

Sung by Mrs. Wilson Northcott at Gaultois, Hermitage Bay, 22nd July 1930.
Mrs. Northcott said that any number of objects could be added.

89 THE TWELVE APOSTLES

Last stanza

I will sing you a twelve-O. What is your twelve-O?

Twelve is the twelve a - post - les, 'Le-ven is the 'le-ven that went to heav'n, Ten is the ten com - mand - ments, Nine of them do shine so bright, Eight is the He-brew chil - dren, Sev'n is the sev'n stars in the skies, Six are the Che-ru-bim wea - vers, Five are the flim - bos un - der the sun, Four are the Gos - pel preach - ers, Three of them were ty - pers, Two of them were li - ly white babes, All robed in green O; One is the one— left a - lone, And e - ver - more shall be so.

I will sing you a one-O.
What is your one-O?

One is the one left alone,
And evermore shall be so.

Last stanza
I will sing you a twelve-O.
What is your twelve-O?

Twelve is the twelve apostles,

251

CUMULATIVE SONGS

Eleven is the eleven that went to heaven,
Ten is the ten commandments,
Nine of them do shine so bright,
Eight is the Hebrew children,
Seven is the seven stars in the skies,
Six are the Cherubim weavers,
Five are the flimbos under the sun,
Four are the Gospel preachers,
Three of them were typers,
Two of them were lily-white babes,
All robed in green-O,
One is the one left alone,
And evermore shall be so.

Sung by Mrs. Violet (John) McCabe at North River, Conception Bay,
16th October 1929

DANCES

DANCES

I had but little opportunity of investigating the dances which are a popular pastime in Newfoundland. The only occasion on which I saw and took part in them was at an evening party given in my honour on 29th September 1929, at Stock Cove, Bonavista Bay, in the house of Mr. James Heaney, where the members of the company were all of Irish descent. In addition to the Cushion Dance, described below, there were 'Sets' and Reels (a type of Square Dance). The dancing was distinguished by the magnificent stepping of the men. This was tremendously rhythmic and vigorous and also very individual which made it almost impossible to note. The role of the girls was rather passive. They stood most of the time holding their partner's hand in a somewhat lackadaisical manner.

Quadrilles and longways dances 'for as many as will' (see p. 258) were also performed in Newfoundland, but I did not see these.

A lively description of Newfoundland dancing is given by Mrs. Greenleaf.[1]

---

[1] Op. cit., p. 13.

1 THE CUSHION DANCE

OR

THE KISSING DANCE

There was an old woman lived in Athlone,
Lived in Athlone, lived in Athlone,
There was an old woman lived in Athlone,
She had one daughter to marry at home.

Now dear daughter [*or* son], choose your mate, *etc.*
Choose a good one, or else choose none.

Sung by Mr. P. K. Devine at St. John's, 11th September 1929

This was my introduction to the folk music of Newfoundland. Soon after my arrival, Mr. P. K. Devine, harbour master, was kind enough to visit me in the Newfoundland Hotel, St. John's, where I was staying. We met in the public lounge, where with complete unselfconsciousness he sang me the song and described the action, at one point dramatically kneeling in front of me. A few days later I took part in this and other dances at Stock Cove, Bonavista Bay (see above).

On this occasion the dance was accompanied by a tune of little value played on the accordion and the dancers did not sing. The action of the dance is as follows:

A member of the company, holding a handkerchief, walks round the room. He stands in front of the lady of his choice, putting the handkerchief in front of her face and kisses her (or sometimes, more modestly, the handkerchief). She then takes the handkerchief from him and places herself in front of him; they walk round the room, the man placing his hands on her shoulders. The woman then chooses a man in like manner, who takes up his position in front of her. And so on until the file is complete, everyone in the room having been chosen.

THE CUSHION DANCE

In the second part, the dancers take hands and form a ring, while the last one who was chosen, and who has the handkerchief, sits down on a chair in the centre of the ring. After a while he chooses a girl from the ring, kisses her and gives her the handkerchief. She takes his place on the chair, while he stands on one side. The girl chooses a man in like manner and so on until all the dancers have been chosen from the ring.

Originally the dancers used to carry a cushion on which the dancer knelt before his or her choice, but in more recent times a handkerchief was substituted for the cushion. Gradually the kneeling has dropped out and the handkerchief is no longer put to its original use.

This dance, if one can call it such, was at one time very popular in England, and also presumably in Ireland.

William Chappell (*Popular Music of the Olden Time*, i, pp. 153–5) gives an interesting historical account of the dance which was, he says, 'in favour both in court and country, and is occasionally danced even at the present day' (i.e. the mid-nineteenth century). He gives many literary references and a description of the dance from the *Dancing Master* of 1686. This is reprinted in Thomas Wilson's *A Companion to the Ball Room*, 1886. The description of the movements accords very closely with the dance as it used to be performed in Newfoundland.

It is perhaps of interest to recount that I took part in the dance in August 1962 when I visited the Tristan da Cunha Islanders at Calshot, near Southampton, where they were living after their evacuation from Tristan on account of the volcanic eruption which had occurred on the island. The dance was spoken of as 'The Pillow Dance', and the second part was called 'The Chair Dance'.

COUNTRY DANCES

I did not see either of the following dances performed, but the movements were described to me. Dance notations are given in *Twelve Traditional Dances* collected and described by Maud Karpeles (Novello, London, 1931).

2 THE SELF

Played by Mr. Dick Penny at Burin, Placentia Bay, 13th July 1930. Mr. Penny always played A music to finish with, although the dance ends with B music. I could not, therefore, discover whether he would have altered the last bar of B music so as to finish on the tonic had he been accompanying the dance.

3 KITTY'S RAMBLES

Sung by Mr. Gordon Cheeseman at Marystown, Placentia Bay, 12th July 1930

258

NOTES ON THE SONGS
AND
BIBLIOGRAPHY

NOTES ON THE SONGS

The references at the head of each note refer to works, listed in the bibliography (pp. 292–4), in which versions of the song have been published. Many of these works contain particulars of additional published versions as well as extensive notes on the songs. We have not therefore attempted to give exhaustive reference to all published versions of the song in our notes and we have reduced to a minimum information on the song which is to be found in other publications. We have not, for instance, normally given specific references to the versions of the Child ballads which are to be found in the comprehensive work of Bronson (Nos. 1–21 of the present collection). Extensive references are all to be found in the bibliographical works of COFFIN and LAWS.

We have endeavoured to give some indication of the geographical distribution of the songs by means of the references and in particular we have made a point of referring to published versions collected in Canada.

Unless otherwise stated, the reference given is to the number of the song and not to the page number. In the page reference the first page only is given when a song (and notes relating to it) cover more than one page.

1 The Outlandish Knight

References:

CHILD, 4; BRONSON i (143 tunes); BROWN N. Carolina ii and iv, 2; DAVIS Virginia, 4; FLANDERS New England 1, p. 82; FOWKE Ontario, 40; GREENLEAF Newfoundland, 1; PEACOCK Newfoundland, p. 206. (COFFIN).

This ballad is widely distributed throughout Europe. The large number of tunes in BRONSON is evidence of its popularity in England and America. Our tune is akin to several of those in Bronson's Group A.

The expression 'meelyer bright' in stanza 8 is puzzling. It may possibly be a corruption of 'milk-white' (steed), although it is improbable that such a well-known expression would have been misunderstood. In a corresponding line in PEACOCK there occurs the equally incomprehensible expression 'a-Nellie Bride'.

2 Earl Brand

References:

CHILD, 7; BRONSON i (40 tunes); BROWN N. Carolina ii and iv, 3; DAVIS Virginia, 5; FLANDERS New England, p. 128. Text without tune is given in GREENLEAF Newfoundland (No. 2). (COFFIN). Was published with pf. accompaniment in KARPELES Newfoundland ii, 2.

NOTES ON THE SONGS

3 The Bonny Banks of Virgie-O

References:

CHILD, 14; BRONSON i (8 tunes); DAVIS Virginia, 9; FLANDERS New England i, p. 213. (COFFIN). One variant is given in GREENLEAF Newfoundland, 4, and two in PEACOCK Newfoundland, p. 809, the second of which was noted from the same singer as our variant A. A was published with pf. accompaniment in KARPELES Newfoundland ii, 1.

4 Hind Horn

References:

CHILD, 17; BRONSON i (23 tunes); FLANDERS New England i, p. 223; FOWKE Ontario, 32; GREENLEAF Newfoundland, 5. (COFFIN). A was published with pf. accompaniment in KARPELES Newfoundland ii, 5.

5 The Cruel Mother

References:

CHILD, 20; BRONSON i (57 tunes); DAVIS Virginia, 12; Flanders New England i, p. 230. (COFFIN). I noted 10 tunes in Newfoundland; and others are given in GREENLEAF Newfoundland, 6, and PEACOCK Newfoundland, p. 804. A was published with pf. accompaniment in KARPELES Newfoundland i, 2.

Bronson has remarked with good reason that 'for the number of beautiful melodic variations on a basically constant rhythmic pattern this ballad is exceptional'. One might, in fact, say that the ballad almost invariably attracts a good tune; or at least enhances the tune that accompanies it, as in tune G, which is the well-known 'The Girl I left behind me'.

Miss Gilchrist in J.F.S.S. vi, p. 80, has an interesting note showing how this ballad and other fragments of traditional verse have been incorporated in children's singing-games.

6 Captain Wedderburn's Courtship

References:

CHILD, 46; BRONSON i (26 tunes); BROWN N. Carolina ii and iv, 12; FLANDERS New England i, p. 299; J.E.F.D.S.S. vii, p. 243 (collected in Ireland); LEACH Labrador, 3. (COFFIN).

This ballad has much in common with other 'riddle' ballads, particularly with 'The Elfin Knight' (CHILD, 2).

NOTES ON THE SONGS

7 Lord Bateman

References:

CHILD, 53; BRONSON i (112 tunes); BROWN N. Carolina ii and iv, 14; DAVIS Virginia, 16; FLANDERS New England ii, p. 9. (COFFIN). I noted 5 tunes in Newfoundland; a text without tune is given in GREENLEAF Newfoundland, 7, and with tune in PEACOCK Newfoundland, p. 210. A was published with pf. accompaniment in KARPELES Newfoundland ii, 3.

Bronson in commenting on the popularity of this ballad gives a penetrating dissertation on the influence of the broadside press on oral transmission. His note should be read in full, but one cannot refrain from quoting a couple of passages: 'The occasional discovery', he writes, 'of a good many manuscript collections of "song-ballets" among undeniably "folk" singers provides further evidence of a practice which, while it can have done little to increase the poetic merit of these old things, must yet have done much to prevent the extremes of mutilation by dullness and forgetfulness, and must often have enabled them to survive at all.' And then the other side of the picture: 'Of course, the breath of life itself lay in the music, which made him [the singer] keep the songs in mind and perpetuated oral transmission.'

8 Fair Margaret and Sweet William

References:

CHILD, 74; BRONSON ii (79 tunes); FLANDERS New England ii, p. 122. PEACOCK Newfoundland, p. 383. (COFFIN).

It was unmistakably a 'swan' and not the more familiar 'swine' that figured in Knight William's dream. The only other version in which a swan is mentioned appears to be in Bronson's variant 38, noted in Kentucky.

9 Sweet William's Ghost

References:

CHILD, 77; BRONSON ii (11 tunes of which all but two are from the present Newfoundland collection); FLANDERS New England ii, p. 178 (from nineteenth-century literary sources, without tune). A text without tune is given in GREENLEAF Newfoundland, 9, and texts with tunes in LEACH Labrador, 4, and PEACOCK Newfoundland, p. 390. (COFFIN).

With the possible exception of a version collected in North Carolina (see BROWN ii and iv, 23) this ballad does not appear to have survived outside Newfoundland. Considering its beauty and dramatic quality this is surprising.

10 The Unquiet Grave

References:

CHILD, 78; BRONSON ii (43 tunes); BROWN N. Carolina ii, 24 (no tune); DAVIS Virginia, 22 (no tune); FLANDERS New England ii, p. 184; 2 tunes are given in GREENLEAF Newfoundland, 10, and 2 in PEACOCK Newfoundland, p. 410. (COFFIN). See also a note by Ruth Harvey (J.E.F.D.S.S. iv, p. 49) on the supernatural implications of these and other analogous ballads.

The last two lines seem to have little connection with the rest of the ballad, but a version from Buchan's MSS. (CHILD D) throws some light on their obscurity. Here the dead man responds as follows to his lover's laments:

> Lament nae mair for me, my love,
> The powers we must obey;
> But hoist up one sail to the wind,
> Your ship must sail away.

In CHILD A, noted in Sussex, the last stanza is:

> The stalk is withered dry, my love,
> So will our hearts decay;
> So make yourself content, my love,
> Till God calls you away.

In a version noted by Cecil Sharp in Somerset the last two lines are:

> And since I lost my own sweetheart
> What can I do but mourn.

11 Matthy Groves

References:

CHILD, 81; BRONSON ii (74 tunes); FLANDERS New England ii, p. 195; LEACH Labrador, 5; PEACOCK Newfoundland, p. 613. (COFFIN).

This ballad, which is widely diffused on the North American continent, has all but disappeared in Great Britain. Cecil Sharp noted only one version in England and that in London from an Irish singer (see BRONSON, variant 25).

Matthy Groves's visit to the 'play-house' instead of the church to hear some 'funny words', which occurs in A, is an unusual variation. Mr. Snow said he had learned the ballad from an English sailor on the Labrador. One wonders whether the English sailor had perpetrated a conscious travesty.

12 George Collins

References:
CHILD, 85; BRONSON ii (43 tunes); PEACOCK Newfoundland, p. 738. (COFFIN).

The connection of this ballad with 'Clerk Colvill' (CHILD, 42) has been much discussed: see note in J.F.S.S. iv, p. 106, by Barbara M. Cra'ster, Bayard in *Journal of American Folklore* lviii (April–June 1945), DAVIS Virginia, p. 199, and BRONSON. The present version is very close to that collected by G. B. Gardiner in Hampshire in 1906, the version on which Miss M. Cra'ster's argument in favour of the relationship of the two ballads is mainly based. We print this version below for the sake of comparison. 'Watching' in the first stanza of our version is probably a corruption of 'washing'.

> George Collins walked out one May morning
> When may was all in bloom.
> 'Twas then he beheld a fair, pretty maid,
> She was washing her marble stone.
>
> She whooped, she holloed, she highered her voice
> And she held up her lily-white hand.
> Come hither to me, George Collins, said she,
> For thy life shall not last you long.
>
> George Collins rode home to his father's own gate,
> And loudly he did ring.
> Come, rise, my dear father, and let me in,
> Come, rise, my dear mother, and make my bed.
>
> . . . .
> . . . .
> All for to trouble my dear sister
> For a napkin to bind round my head.
>
> For, if I chance to die this night,
> As I suppose I shall,

Bury me under that marble stone
That's against fair Helen's hall.

Fair Helen doth sit in her room so fine,
Working her silken skein;
Then she saw the first corpse a-coming
As ever the sun shined on.

She said unto her Irish maid:
Whose corpse is this so fine?
This is George Collins's corpse a-coming,
That once was a true lover of thine.

You go upstairs and fetch me the sheet
That's wove with a silver twine
And hang that over George Collins's head,
Tomorrow it shall hang over mine.

This news was carried to fair London town,
And wrote all on fair London gate;
Six pretty maids died all of one night,
And all for George Collins's sake.

13 Lamkin

References:
CHILD, 93; BRONSON ii (30 tunes); DAVIS Virginia, 28 (no tune);
FLANDERS New England, p. 296; LEACH Labrador, 6; PEACOCK Newfoundland, p. 806. (COFFIN). Tune B was published with pf. accompaniment in KARPELES Newfoundland i, 4.

Miss Broadwood (J.F.S.S. v, p. 84) states that she has seen what is said to be the original Lankin's (or Lonkin's) tower close to the little village of Ovingham-on-Tyne in Northumberland. It was then a mere shell, overgrown with underwood.

Attention should be called to Miss Gilchrist's article in J.E.F.D.S.S. i, p. 1, in which she traces the evolution of two separate traditions: one Scottish and the other Northumbrian.

14 Willie o' Winsbury

References:
CHILD, 100; BRONSON ii (22 tunes). (COFFIN). Three versions are

NOTES ON THE SONGS

given in GREENLEAF Newfoundland, 13; 2 in LEACH Labrador, 7, and 2 in PEACOCK Newfoundland, p. 534. A was published with pf. accompaniment in KARPELES Newfoundland i, 5.

The name of the hero is often Young Barbour, or Willie or Thomas Barber.

15 The Bailiff's Daughter of Islington
References:
CHILD, 105; BRONSON ii (34 tunes). (COFFIN).

16 The Baffled Knight
References:
CHILD, 112; BRONSON ii (33 tunes, including 8 under the title of 'The New Mown Hay' which are relegated to an Appendix); PEACOCK Newfoundland, p. 272. (COFFIN).

This ballad is closely related to 'The Knight and the Shepherd's Daughter' (CHILD, 110). Only one stanza of the text was noted and it is therefore difficult to know with certainty which of the two titles should be attributed to this fragment. It would seem, however, that in 'The Baffled Knight' the initial emphasis is usually placed on the male character as in our version, whereas in 'The Knight and the Shepherd's Daughter' it is the shepherdess who first appears on the scene.

For a good singable text, see SHARP English F.S. ii, 3. If this is used the refrain of the Newfoundland version should be retained.

17 The Gypsy Laddie
References:
CHILD, 200; BRONSON iii (128 tunes); BARRY Maine, 33; BROWN N. Carolina ii and iv, 37; CREIGHTON Traditional Nova Scotia, p. 71; DAVIS Virginia, 33; EDDY Ohio, 21; FOWKE Ontario, 3; GREENLEAF Newfoundland, 16; MORRIS Florida, 166; PEACOCK Newfoundland, p. 184; SHARP Appalachian i, 33; SHARP English F.S. i, 5. (COFFIN). The A tune with composite text was published with pf. accompaniment in KARPELES Newfoundland i, 3.

18 Sir James The Ross
References:
CHILD, 213; BRONSON iii (27 tunes); BARRY Maine, 36; CREIGH-

TON Maritime Nova Scotia, p. 23; CREIGHTON Traditional Nova
Scotia, p. 75; GREIG Aberdeen, 64; MACKENZIE Nova Scotia, 11 (2
texts without tune); PEACOCK Newfoundland, p. 715. (COFFIN).

Alexander Keith, the editor of *Last Leaves* (GREIG Aberdeen), supplies
a valuable note on the history of this ballad. He points out that there
are two extant versions: the one traditional and the other literary. In
the North East of Scotland the literary versions has to a great extent
ousted the traditional version. Dr. Keith is of the opinion that the texts
of both versions are derived from stall copies, broadsides, etc. of the second
half of the eighteenth century. He published the earliest text he has
seen, taken from *A Collection of One Hundred and Fifty Scots Songs* (printed
for A. Millar, London, 1768). This text was reprinted on several occa-
sions and was, no doubt incorrectly, attributed to the poet Michael
Bruce (1746–67). Our text A, as well as those of Barry, Creighton
(Traditional) and Mackenzie are very close to the version printed in
1768. The Barry version was taken from a manuscript in the possession
of the singer who also had a printed copy. The existence of printed
copies might account indirectly for the completeness of the Nova Scotia
and Newfoundland versions.

The few obscurities in our A text can be made intelligible by reference
to the following lines from the 1768 version printed in GREIG Aberdeen:

[1]1.4	That knight of muckle fame.
2.2	His growth was as the tufted fir
3	That crowns the mountains' brow.
4.1	In bloody fight, thrice had he stood
7.1	At last she blessed his well try'd faith
8.4	A blooming saugh tree stood.
10.1	Thus the maid began: My sire
2	Your passion disapproves
15.3	For [Daniel's] blade before his breast
4	Had pierced, *etc.*
19.1	Thro' the green woods he quickly hy'd
21.4	That can assist their lord.
29.3	Dishonour blast my name! But he
4	By me ere morning dies.
31.1	They spurred their steeds in furious moves

[1] The numbers refer to the stanzas and lines of our A text.

33.3 He furious pricked his sweaty steed

34.2 If horse and man hold good

35.4 From whence I hoped thine aid.

39. Oft boasting hides a coward's heart,
    My weighty sword you fear,
    Which shone in front in Flodden field
    When you kept in the rear.

40.3 Then Graham gave back, and fear'd his arm,

47.2 By death's arrest denied.
   3 My race is run. Adieu, my love!

19 The Dowie Dens of Yarrow

References:
CHILD, 214; BRONSON iii (42 tunes); FOWKE Ontario, 23; GREIG Aberdeen, 65. (COFFIN).

Gavin Greig has said that 'no ballad is better known in Aberdeenshire'. It has not been collected south of the border except from Scottish informants.

Our text is very close to the many versions that have been noted, but it lacks the moving description of the girl's finding the body of her true love. To complete the story we give below the last five stanzas of the text as noted by Gavin Greig:

As she gaed ower yon high high hill,
An' down yon den so narrow,
'Twas there she saw her true love John
A-bleedin sair in Yarrow.

She washed his face, she combed his hair,
As she had done before O,
An' she kissed the blood off fae his wounds
In the dowie dens o' Yarrow.

Her hair was full three quarters lang,
An' the colour o' it was yellow:
She tied it round his middle sae sma,
An' she carried him hame to Yarrow.

Out it spoke her old father:
What need for a' this sorrow?

I'll wed ye to a better man
Than the one ye lost in Yarrow.

O father dear, ye hae seven sons,
Ye may wed them a' tomorrow,
But a fairer flower ne'er sprang in June
Than the one I lost in Yarrow.

'Carrow' which occurs in the last line of stanza 4 is an obsolete Irish word signifying a company of itinerant gamblers (see O.E.D.). It is possible that the text has become confused and that 'carrow' refers to the nine hired men who were lying in wait for the hero.

It is also possible that 'carrow' is a corruption of 'Curragh' (as in No. 54, 'The Winter's gone and Past').

20 The Green Wedding

References:
CHILD, 221; BRONSON iii (11 tunes); BARRY Maine, 8, p. 400; CREIGHTON Songs Nova Scotia, p. 22; CREIGHTON Traditional Nova Scotia, p. 79; GREIG Aberdeen, p. 71; SHARP English F.S. i, 16. (COFFIN, p. 133).

The history of this ballad and its connection with Katharine Jaffray is very perplexing. Child gives a full account of its various appearances in manuscript and print, including Sir Walter Scott's re-fashioning of the ballad. In his head-notes, Child refers to 'a copy from the recitation of a young Irishwoman living in Taunton, Massachusetts (learned from print, I suppose, and in parts imperfectly remembered)' and proceeds to give the story of the ballad which we know as 'The Green Wedding', quoting half a dozen stanzas. Also in his L version from the Macmath MS., 'communicated January 13, 1883, by Dr. Robert Trotter, as remembered from the recitation of his father, Dr. Robert Trotter of Dalry, Kirkcudbrightshire', two stanzas are given which include the lines:

O I saw nocht but a fairy troop,
As I rode on my way.

And he adds the following note: 'The story of the ballad was that Lochinvar went to Netherby with a band of men dressed in green . . . with whose assistance he forcibly abducted the young lady.' Child evidently regarded this and the recitation of the young Irishwoman as versions, or at least a re-fashioning of the Kathering Jaffray ballad and this opinion is endorsed both by Barry and Coffin. Barry in the section devoted to Secondary Ballads gives two texts. One of them, which was from an informant who had learned it as a child in Waterford, Ireland, corresponds to Child's Irish text, of which the original was found in the Williams Collection of Irish Broadsides in the Public Library of Providence, R.I., and the other, which was recited by a native of New Brunswick, corresponds to Child's L text. Sharp, in considering the relationship of the two types, writes: 'Whether our ballad is a corrupt and incomplete version of the Scottish one it is difficult to say. Although the two have several lines in common, there is something in the plot of "The Green Wedding" which, despite its obscurity, seems to indicate a motive which is absent from "Katherine Janfaire". The scheme of our story seems to turn upon the dressing in green of both hero and heroine at the wedding-feast.' Sharp records that the ballad was sung to a very poor tune and that he therefore selected another tune to accompany the ballad. His original tune is a variant of ours, which is related to 'The Banks of the Sweet Dundee'.

I noted in Newfoundland three more variants of the tune—even less distinguished than the one given above—and two more texts. In these, Amber Town or Amberley Town, as given as the place of the wedding and in one of the texts the lass comes from Belfast.

In none of the Newfoundland texts is the situation clearly described in the opening lines. The first stanza of Barry's text makes for clarity.

> There was a lord and a wealthy lord,
> A lord of high renown,
> He courted a North Country lass
> Until he had her won.
> And when her parents came to know
> Quite angry they grew;
> It was their delight, both day and night,
> To keep her from off his view.

21 The Lover's Ghost

References:

CHILD, 248; BARRY Maine, 44 (no tune); CREIGHTON Traditional Nova Scotia, p. 83; JOYCE Irish, 408; SHARP Appalachian, 36. (COFFIN). A was published with pf. accompaniment in KARPELES Newfoundland ii, 7.

It is questionable whether one is justified in attributing this ballad to 'The Grey Cock', for in the one version from Herd given by Child there is no indication that Johnny, who visits his lover, is a ghost. However, Barry, whose version is similar to that of Child, has the imagination to perceive that 'the crowing of a cock in any old song . . . warns the ballad hunter that ghosts are near'. And he quotes Joyce's 'The Lover's Ghost' which must, he says, stand as the original of 'The Grey Cock'. Joyce's text is very close to ours, except that the role of the lovers is reversed and the ghostly night visitor is a woman. In the two versions published by Dr. Creighton, there seems to be some confusion. Johnny, apparently a living man, visits his true love Margaret in her own home and it is inferred that she is a ghost: a most unusual situation. In SHARP Appalachian, there is no indication that the visiting lover is a *revenant*.

22 Henry Martin

References:
CHILD, 250; BARRY Maine, 29; BROADWOOD English Traditional, p. 30; CREIGHTON Traditional Nova Scotia, p. 86; DAVIS Virginia, 37 (no tune); EDDY Ohio, 24; J.F.S.S. i, p. 162; iv, pp. 92 and 301; and viii, p. 182; SHARP English F.S. i, 1. (COFFIN). A was published with pf. accompaniment in KARPELES Newfoundland ii, 6.

Here one is met with the controversial subject of whether or not this is the same ballad as 'Sir Andrew Barton' (CHILD, 167). It is not proposed to relate here all details of the controversy; these can be found in the various publications listed above. Briefly, Child is of opinion that this ballad sprang from the ashes of 'Sir Andrew Barton', and this theory is borne out by Barry in a note on the three texts which he gives under the title of 'Sir Andrew Barton'. The argument is well summed up, but perhaps not definitely resolved, by Davis. Sharp regarded the two ballads as distinct, but he did not know of the American versions which may provide a link.

The present versions and those collected by Dr. Creighton in Nova Scotia conform to the normal 'Henry Martin' type. Our three versions are very similar to others that have been collected in England.

23 The Golden Vanity

References:
CHILD, 286; BARRY Maine, 52; BROWN N. Carolina ii and iv, 47; CREIGHTON Songs Nova Scotia, 20; DAVIS Virginia, 43; FOWKE Ontario, 4 and 61; GREENLEAF Newfoundland, 19; GREIG Aberdeen, 101; LEACH Labrador, 8; MORRIS Florida, 174 (no tune); SHARP Appalachian i, 41; SHARP English F.S. i, 14. (COFFIN).

NOTES ON THE SONGS

This is one of the most popular sea-songs on both sides of the Atlantic. Curiously, I came across only this one tune with a fragmentary text which I did not note. Fragments only without tune were noted by Mrs. Greenleaf.

24 Pretty Sally

References:
CHILD, 295; BARRY Maine, p. 418; BELDEN Missouri, p. 111; BROWN N. Carolina ii and iv, 90; J.F.S.S. viii, p. 5; JOYCE Irish, 153; SHARP Appalachian i, 44. (COFFIN).

It is questionable whether this ballad should be listed as Child, 295. Most American scholars regard it as a separate ballad and its title is usually given as 'The [Rich] Irish Lady'. It is true that the characters are reversed and that in the Child version it is the man and not the girl who falls sick, but there are certain common motives, particularly the dancing on the grave and the rings she took from off her hand. There is also the reference to sending for the doctor in Child's B version. We therefore think that there is sufficient justification for regarding this as the Child ballad, although, following the example of Barry, it might properly be designated as a 'Secondary Ballad'.

The present text is very close to 'Sally and her True Love Billy', a broadside in the Yale University Library which is reprinted by Barry. The missing lines from stanza 3 might be supplied from this text. They are:

> So keep your intentions and hold your discourse,
> For I never will [love] you unless I am forced.

25 The Bloody Gardener

This was published with pf. accompaniment in KARPELES Newfoundland i, 7.

A more sophisticated broadside version with twenty-seven stanzas is to be found in the Harvard University Library in a fourteen-volume collection of ballads printed by Catnach, Bebbington, Ryle, etc. An extract is quoted in Brand's *Popular Antiquities*, iii, p. 217 (1893 ed.). Another similar version, entitled 'The Bloody Gardener's Cruelty', or 'The Shepherd's Daughter Betrayed', is in a chapbook, printed at Tewkesbury at the beginning of the century by S. Harrow. A relative of his, an old lady of over ninety, used to sing the ballad (see J. Harvey Bloom's *Folk Lore in Shakespeare Land*), but it was not noted from her, the only other version with tune that has so far come to light is to be found in PEACOCK Newfoundland, p. 668.

NOTES ON THE SONGS

26 Shooting of His Dear
References:
BROWN N. Carolina ii and iv, 76; Bulletin of North East x, p. 12;
CREIGHTON Maritime Nova Scotia, p. 111; GARDNER Michigan, 14;
HUDSON Mississippi, 32; J.E.F.D.S.S. vii, p. 241 (collected in Ireland);
J.F.S.S. ii, p. 59; vii, p. 17; JOYCE Irish, 409; MORRIS Florida, 214;
O'LOCHLAINN Irish Street Ballads, 29; PETRIE Irish, 724 and 1171;
SHARP Appalachian i, 50. (LAWS, p. 243, O 36).

This ballad, which is popular both on the North American continent
and in the British Isles, is believed to be Gaelic—probably Irish—in
origin. Sharp writes (J.F.S.S. ii, p. 60): 'The incidents related in the song
are a strange admixture of fancy with matter of fact. I would hazard
the suggestion that the ballad is the survival of a genuine piece of Celtic
or, still more probably, of Norse imagination, and that the efforts made
to account for the tragedy without resorting to the supernatural . . .
are the work of a more modern and less imaginative generation of
singers.' Still, the fact remains that Molly (or Polly) still appears at the
trial (or, in our version, to her lover's uncle) in the form of a swan. In
some versions she appears as a 'mountain of snow'.
The reader is referred to important notes by Barry (Bulletin) and
Gilchrist (J.F.S.S. vii, p. 17) on the mythological aspects of the ballad.
The present tune, which is not the usual one, commonly accompanies
'The Duke of Bedford' (see SHARP English F.S. ii, 5).

27 The Cruel Ship's Carpenter
References:
BROWN ii and iv, 64; CREIGHTON Traditional Nova Scotia, p. 114;
J.F.S.S. i, p. 172; LEACH Labrador, 20; PEACOCK Newfoundland, p. 404;
RANDOLPH ii, 153; SHARP Appalachian ii, 49 (LAWS, p. 268, P 36).

28 The Sea Captain
References:
BELDEN Missouri, p. 107; Bulletin of Northeast vii, p. 12; CREIGH-
TON Maritime Nova Scotia, p. 41; GREENLEAF Newfoundland, 28;
JOYCE Irish, 327; MACKENZIE Nova Scotia, 74; PEACOCK Newfound-
land, p. 296 (LAWS, p. 154, K 27). Tunes A and B were published
with pf. accompaniment in KARPELES Newfoundland i, 6.

We would have suspected that the heroine of this ballad was no ordinary maid and our suspicions are confirmed by Joyce, who gives a similar tune and one stanza, 'O were my men drunk', etc., to which is prefixed a note giving his informant's description of the story in the following words: 'A beautiful mermaid visited a ship by moonlight. The captain tried to detain her, but she chanted a song that threw captain and crew into a trance and so she escaped.'

Barry in *Bulletin of the Northeast* gives many European analogues.

29 Still Growing

References:

CREIGHTON Maritime Nova Scotia, p. 100; CREIGHTON Traditional Nova Scotia, p. 107; J.F.S.S. i, p. 214; ii, pp. 44, 95, 206 and 274; v, p. 190; PEACOCK Newfoundland, p. 677; SHARP Appalachian i, 72; SHARP English F.S. ii, 9. (LAWS, p. 242, O 35).

This is perhaps the most beautiful of all ballads outside the Child canon. It is not current to any great extent on the North American continent and the tunes found there are not, generally speaking, as fine as their British counterparts.

'Old hanks of vine', in the first line of the penultimate stanza, may be a corruption of 'holland so fine' which occurs in many other versions.

30 The Nobleman's Wedding

References:

ASHTON Street Ballads, p. 173; BELDEN Missouri, p. 165 (no tune); CREIGHTON Maritime Nova Scotia, p. 80; CREIGHTON Traditional Nova Scotia, p. 126 (tune only) and p. 158 (text only); GREENLEAF Newfoundland, 75; J.F.S.S. viii, pp. 4, 37 and 202; JOYCE Irish, 90 and 413; PEACOCK Newfoundland, p. 691; PETRIE Irish, 490–5; SHARP Appalachian ii, 105. (LAWS, p. 264, P 31). Has been published with pf. accompaniment in KARPELES Newfoundland ii, 14.

In J.F.S.S. viii, pp. 202–6, Miss Gilchrist discusses the connection of this song with the serio-comic song of the 1830's (see ASHTON). The two texts in CREIGHTON Maritime give no story, but are laments for a departed lover.

31 The False Bride

References:

J.F.S.S. i, p. 23; ii, p. 12 (with references to other sources including ballad-sheets); PEACOCK Newfoundland, p. 441.

NOTES ON THE SONGS

This was a popular song in Newfoundland. In addition to the three examples noted, I heard it many times: often sung by a party of young men in chorus as they were walking homewards of an evening.

I know of no version extant in other regions of North America, but it is possible that I have missed some references.

32 Edwin in the Lowlands Low

References:
BELDEN Missouri, p. 127 (no tune); BROWN N. Carolina ii and iv, 79; CREIGHTON Traditional Nova Scotia, p. 220; MACKENZIE Nova Scotia, 27 (no tune); J.F.S.S. i, p. 124; iii, p. 266; viii, p. 227 (this last was noted in Ontario); J. Irish F.S.S. iii, 24; PEACOCK Newfoundland, p. 641; RANDOLPH Ozark ii, 140; SHARP Appalachian i, 56; SHARP English County, p. 136. (LAWS, p. 197, M 34).

33 The Three Butchers

References:
BROWN N. Carolina ii and iv, 80; GREENLEAF Newfoundland, 37; J.F.S.S. i, p. 174; viii, p. 2; LEACH Labrador, 59; MORRIS Florida, 207; PEACOCK Newfoundland, p. 817; RANDOLPH Ozark i, 97; SHARP Appalachian i, 60. (LAWS, p. 166, L 4).

The earliest known printed version is a seventeenth-century broadside (see Miss Broadwood in J.F.S.S. i, p. 174, and LAWS).

34 A Health to the King

This would appear to be of Irish origin. I have not found any other version.

35 The Turkish Lady

References:
CREIGHTON Songs Nova Scotia, 13; MACKENZIE Nova Scotia, 17 (no tune); SHARP English County, p. 214. (LAWS, p. 238, O 26).

36 The Bold Lieutenant

References:
CREIGHTON Maritime Nova Scotia, p. 34; CREIGHTON Songs Nova Scotia, 43; J.F.S.S. v, p. 258; LEACH Labrador, 32; MACKENZIE Nova Scotia, 22; SHARP Appalachian i, 66; SHARP F.S. Somerset iii, 56. (LAWS, p. 237, O 25).

NOTES ON THE SONGS

Sharp states in J.F.S.S. and in F.S. Somerset that the earliest version of the story known to him is in *Les Memoires de Messire Pierre de Bourdeille, Seigneur de Brantôme* (1666), who relates it as a true story of M. de Lorge (François de Montgommery) who at the behest of his mistress, a lady at the court of François Ier (1585-1647) entered a lion's den and recovered her glove. Brantôme's anecdote is quoted in Saintfoix's *Essais historiques sur Paris* (1766) and it is from this source that Schiller derived his poem *Der Handschuh* (1797). Other writers, including Robert Browning, have used the same story. In the French versions of the tale, the hero, having recovered the glove, casts his mistress aside in disgust at the task she had imposed upon him. Cecil Sharp believed that the folk tradition was of earlier date than Brantôme's story. He mentions that lions were kept at the Tower of London from the reign of Henry I down to 1834.

37 The Councillor's Daughter
References:
CREIGHTON Songs Nova Scotia, 24; FLANDERS Green Mountain, p. 121; SHARP Appalachian i, 68. (LAWS, p. 216, N 26).
The tune is reminiscent of 'The Gypsy Laddie' (SHARP Appalachian i, 33 D).

38 Jack in London City
References:
Bulletin of Northeast iii, p. 10; FLANDERS New England ii, p. 82; GREENLEAF Newfoundland, 50; J.F.S.S. ii, p. 38; PEACOCK Newfoundland, p. 288; SHARP English County, p. 174. (LAWS, p. 161, K 40).

Barry in *Bulletin of Northeast* suggests that this is a secondary form of 'Glasgerion' (CHILD, 67). In both cases the story relates how a man of inferior birth enters by trickery the bedchamber of another man's mistress, but apart from this the two ballads have nothing in common.

39 The Rich Old Lady
References:
BELDEN Missouri, p. 237 (no tune); BROWN N. Carolina ii and iv, 181 and 182; CREIGHTON Maritime Nova Scotia, p. 122; HUGHES Irish, p. 166; LEACH Labrador, 113; MORRIS Florida, 197; PEACOCK Newfoundland, p. 261; RANDOLPH Ozark iv, 754; SHARP Appalachian i, 55. (LAWS, p. 274, Q 2 and Q 3).

Belden has a valuable note in which he points to two forms of the

277

story. Recent collection shows, however, that the two forms have become intermingled.

40 The Spanish Main

The theme of this song is a familiar one. The only published version I have found is PEACOCK Newfoundland, p. 720.

41 Spanish Ladies

References:
CREIGHTON Traditional Nova Scotia, p. 233; J.F.S.S. ii, p. 179; MACKENZIE Nova Scotia, 97 (no tune); SHARP English F.S. ii, 39.

Sharp writes: 'This is a Capstan Chantey. It is also well known in the Navy, where it is sung as a song, chanteys not being permitted.' The tune noted by him is in the aeolian mode, as is that noted by R. Vaughan Williams in J.F.S.S. Sharp deplores the fact that nowadays 'sailors sing a modernized and far less beautiful form of the air in the major mode'—of which our version is an example. Mr. Day said he had learned the song from a Welshman.

42 The Greenland Fishery

References:
J.F.S.S. i, p. 101; ii, p. 243; viii, p. 279; PEACOCK Newfoundland, p. 147; SHARP Somerset iii, 74 (LAWS, p. 150, K 21).

The sentiment expressed in the penultimate stanza of our text is certainly candid, if somewhat unexpected. ASHTON Street Ballads, p. 265, has similar lines:

> Now the losing of the Prentice boys
> It grieved the captain sore,
> But the losing of the great big whale
> It grieved him very much more.

43 Sweet William

References:
BELDEN Missouri, p. 186; BROWN N. Carolina ii and iv, 104; CREIGHTON Songs Nova Scotia, 27; EDDY Ohio, 33; HUGHES Irish iv, p. 13; J.F.S.S. i, p. 99; ii, p. 293; viii, p. 212; J. Irish F.S.S. xvii, 10;

NOTES ON THE SONGS

LEACH Labrador, 9; O'LOCHLAINN Irish Street Ballads, 56; RAN-
DOLPH Ozark i, 68; SHARP Appalachian ii, 106; SHARP English F.S.
ii, 20 (LAWS, p. 146, K 12). Has been published with pf. accompaniment in KARPELES Newfoundland i, 12.

This song, as will be seen from the above references, is widely distributed in the British Isles and in North America.

44 Arbour Town

References:
BROWN N. Carolina ii and iv, 105; J.F.S.S. iii, p. 258; KIDSON,
p. 112; SHARP English County, p. 162.

In Brown's N. Carolina version as well as in the English versions, the
scene is laid in Scarborough, on the Yorkshire coast (in KIDSON, it is
Stowboro') and the lovers are usually buried in Robin Hood's Churchyard.

Our tune is practically the same as that of 'Floro' (No. 58).

45 Reilly the Fisherman

References:
CREIGHTON Maritime Nova Scotia, p. 102; CREIGHTON Traditional
Nova Scotia, p. 172; GREENLEAF Newfoundland, 90 (no tune);
J.F.S.S. i, p. 256; ii, p. 214; v, p. 147; J. Irish F.S.S. i, p. 5; JOYCE
Irish, 53; LEACH Labrador, 13; MACKENZIE Nova Scotia, 43 (no tune);
PEACOCK Newfoundland, p. 698; SHARP English County, p. 107.
(LAWS, p. 183, M 8). Has been published with pf. accompaniment in
KARPELES Newfoundland i, 14.

This is a popular song, probably of Irish origin.

46 The Simple Ploughboy

References:
BROWN N. Carolina ii, 103 (no tune); CREIGHTON Traditional Nova
Scotia, p. 176; J.F.S.S. i, p. 132; ii, p. 146; iv, p. 303; viii, p. 268;
JOYCE Irish, 412; MACKENZIE Nova Scotia, 45 (no tune); SHARP
Appalachian i, 59; SHARP English County, p. 192. (LAWS, p. 191,
M 24).

47 The Press Gang

References:
CREIGHTON Traditional Nova Scotia, p. 146; J.F.S.S. ii, p. 181;
viii, pp. 9 and 265; LEACH Labrador, 35. (LAWS, p. 204 N 6).

NOTES ON THE SONGS

48 Wearing of the Blue

A close version of the text (with tune) is given in LEACH Labrador, 90, under the title of 'Canadee-I-O'. This song is not the same as 'Canada-I-O' published in Alan Lomax's *The Folk Songs of North America* (London, 1960) and elsewhere.

49 William Taylor

References:

BELDEN Missouri, p. 182 (no tune); BROWN N. Carolina ii and iv, 106; CREIGHTON Songs Nova Scotia, 32; FOWKE Ontario, 60; GREENLEAF Newfoundland, 22; J.F.S.S. i, p. 254; iii, p. 214; v, pp. 68 and 161; J. Irish F.S.S. v, 12; JOYCE Irish, 424; LEACH Labrador, 131; MACKENZIE Nova Scotia, 46 (no tune); PETRIE Irish, 745; RANDOLPH Ozark i, 67; SHARP Appalachian i, 61; SHARP English F.S. i, 50. (LAWS, p. 208, N 11). Has been published with pf. accompaniment in KARPELES Newfoundland ii, 12.

50 The Rose of Britain's Isle

References:

CREIGHTON Songs Nova Scotia, 48; GREENLEAF Newfoundland, 29 (no tune); MACKENZIE Nova Scotia, 37 (no tune). (LAWS, p. 210, N 16). There does not appear to be any traditional version recorded in the British Isles.

There are some words missing in the last half of the final stanza. Creighton gives:

> They married were and bells did ring
> And the villagers did smile.
> Now happy is young Edmund with
> The Rose of Britain's Isle.

And Mackenzie's version is:

> Young Edward lives contented,
> And on each other smile.
> Young Edward he is happy now
> With the Rose of Britain's Isle.

NOTES ON THE SONGS

51 Farewell Nancy

References:

BROWN N. Carolina ii and iv, 101; J.F.S.S. i, p. 130; iii, pp. 99 and 298; JOYCE Irish, 93; SHARP English F.S. i, 26. (LAWS, p. 147, K 14). In one of the N. Carolina versions Nancy witnesses the drowning of her lover.

52 Jimmy and Nancy

References:

BELDEN Missouri, p. 177 (no tune); CREIGHTON Maritime Nova Scotia, p. 66; CREIGHTON Traditional Nova Scotia, p. 156; J.F.S.S. ii, p. 22; vi, p. 17; vii, p. 50; MACKENZIE Nova Scotia, 35 (no tune); PEACOCK Newfoundland, p. 293; SHARP Appalachian ii, 121. (LAWS, p. 206, N 8). This is not the same song as 'Jack Monroe' or 'Jacky Fraser' (LAWS, N 7) although sometimes the two songs are confused.

It will be noted that in text A 'Lewisburg' has been substituted for 'Lisbon'.
A much better text is given in BELDEN (text A). The somewhat confused lines in our text are given as follows:
Stanza 2, lines 3 and 4:
I'll fear no storm or battle, let them be e'er so great,
Like true and faithful servant upon you I will wait.
Stanza 4, line 4:
I'm afraid you would not answer if I on you should call.

53 Nancy of London

References:

GREENLEAF Newfoundland, 33; J.F.S.S. iii, p. 101 and 272; LEACH Labrador, 49; PEACOCK Newfoundland, p. 568; RANDOLPH Ozark i, 78. I noted two other versions in Newfoundland.

54 The Winter's Gone and Past

References:

BROADWOOD English county, p. 104; J.F.S.S. iii, p. 81; JOYCE Irish, 427. Has been published with pf. accompaniment in KARPELES Newfoundland ii, 10.

'Carrow' is doubtless a corruption of 'Curragh'.
J.F.S.S. gives two beautiful variants of the tune, collected in Dorset, as well as notes on the song and other references. According to Miss

Broadwood, the song appears in most Scottish collections. It is among the broadside songs which are included in Herd's (MSS. I, 43 a–b), and it was arranged by Burns for Johnson's *Scots Musical Museum*, 3rd ed. 1853, i, p. 208 (1st ed. 1787–1803). The text of Herd's MS. is reproduced by Hans Hecht in his *Songs from David Herd's Manuscripts* (Edinburgh, 1904), No. CIV. We think it may be of interest to compare this with our version and we therefore give it below. The words in brackets are from the *Roxburghe Ballads*.

1   The winter it is past and the summer's come at last,
    And the small birds sing on every tree;
    The hearts of these are glad while mine is very sad,
    While my true love is absent from me.

2   I wou'd na think it strange the wide world for to range,
    If I cou'd obtain my [heart's] delight,
    But here in Cupid's chain I'm obliged to remain
    And in tears for to spend the whole night.

3   The ribbons I will [A livery I'll] wear and I'll comb doun my hair,
    And I'll dress in the velvet so green,
    Straightway I will repair to the Curicle of Culdair [Curragh of
                                  Kildare]
    And there I'll hear tidings from him.

4   With patience I [she] did wait till he ran for the plate
    Thinking young Johnston for to see,
    But Fortune prov'd unkind to this sweetheart of mine,
    And he's gone to the Logans [Lurgan] from me.

5   All youth that are in love and cannot it remove,
    You pity'd are for to be;
    Experience makes me know that your hearts are full of woe,
    Since it fared once so with me.
    [Since my true love is absent from me.]

6   O my love is like the sun in the firmament doth run,
    That is always both constant and true,
    But yours is like the moon that wanders up and doun:
    [And in] Every month it is new.

7   But farewell my joy and heart, since you and I must part;
    Ye're the fairest of all I do [that e'er I did] see,

I never do design to alter my mind,
Altho' you'r below my degree.

Hecht is of opinion that stanza 2 is Burns's own composition. Miss Gilchrist in J.F.S.S. writes that 'The hero is supposed to have been an Irish highwayman called Johnston, hung about the middle of the eighteenth century for robberies committed in the Curragh of Kildare'.

55 The Dark-eyed Sailor

References:
BROWN N. Carolina ii and iv, 95; CREIGHTON Songs Nova Scotia, 29; CREIGHTON Traditional Nova Scotia, p. 144; FLANDERS Green Mountain, p. 36; FOWKE Ontario, 9; GREENLEAF Newfoundland, 36 (no tune); J.F.S.S. iv, p. 129; O'LOCHLAINN Irish Street Ballads, 5; PEACOCK Newfoundland, p. 513. (LAWS, p. 221, N 35).

This and 'The Broken Token' are among the most popular songs on both sides of the Atlantic.

56 The Pride of Glencoe

References:
CREIGHTON Maritime Nova Scotia, p. 60; GREENLEAF Newfoundland, 86 (no tune); J.F.S.S. ii, p. 171, and v, p. 100; JOYCE Irish, 322; LEACH Labrador, 129; MACKENZIE Nova Scotia, 68; PEACOCK Newfoundland, p. 519. (LAWS, p. 223, N 39).

Miss Broadwood who noted this song in Co. Waterford, Ireland (see J.F.S.S.) thinks it is probably of North Irish or West Highland origin.
Text without tune is given in Gavin Greig's *Folk-Song of the North-East*, Art. LV (reprinted by Folklore Associates, Hatboro, Penn., 1963).
In stanza 6 'enchanting smile' is probably intended. Creighton has:

I said: My pretty fair maid, your enchanting smile
And comely sweet features does my heart beguile.

And Mackenzie's lines are:

I said: My gay lassie, your enchanting smiles
And comely sweet figure does my heart beguile.

57 The Blind Beggar's Daughter of Bethnal Green

References:
GREENLEAF Newfoundland, 32 (no tune); J.F.S.S. i, p. 202;

NOTES ON THE SONGS

SHARP Appalachian i, 46; SHARP English F.S. ii, 16. (LAWS, p. 217, N 27).

Bishop Percy believed this song to have been written in the reign of Elizabeth. The original story is very much longer than the later broadsides (see LAWS).

58 Floro

References:
CREIGHTON Maritime Nova Scotia, p. 82; J.F.S.S. i, p. 90; J. Irish F.S.S. iv, p. 23; PEACOCK Newfoundland, p. 480. A was published with pf. accompaniment in KARPELES Newfoundland ii, 9.

59 A Man in Love

References:
CREIGHTON Traditional Nova Scotia, p. 214.
I am informed by Mr. Hugh Shields that this song is current in Ulster and that he himself has noted versions in County Derry.

60 Proud Nancy

References:
CREIGHTON Traditional Nova Scotia, p. 189. Cf. 'The Rejected Lover' in SHARP Appalachian ii, 109. The present version was published with pf. accompaniment in KARPELES Newfoundland i, 9.

61 The Bleaches so Green

I know of no other version of this song. It would seem to be of Irish origin.

62 The Saucy Sailor

References:
CREIGHTON Traditional Nova Scotia, p. 202; FOWKE Ontario, 8; J.F.S.S. iv, p. 342; SHARP Appalachian ii, 168; SHARP English F.S. i, 29. (LAWS, p. 160, K 38).

The missing word in stanza 6 may possibly be 'lent'.
The first two lines of the last stanza are as follows in many other versions:

Since you've refused the offer, love,
Some other maid shall wear the ring.

NOTES ON THE SONGS

63 Early, Early in the Spring

References:
BELDEN Missouri, p. 163 (no tune); BROWN N. Carolina ii and iv, 87; CREIGHTON Maritime Nova Scotia, p. 98; CREIGHTON Traditional Nova Scotia, p. 154; PEACOCK Newfoundland, p. 549; PETRIE, 765; RANDOLPH Ozark i, 81; SHARP Appalachian ii, 125; SHARP Somerset iii, 70. (LAWS, p. 180, M 1).

64 The Streams of Lovely Nancy

References:
CREIGHTON Maritime Nova Scotia, p. 79; J.F.S.S. i, p. 122; iii, p. 53; iv, p. 310, and vii, p. 59.

There are many broadside versions of this song and they are mostly very corrupt and confused. In J.F.S.S. iv, p. 310, Miss Gilchrist and Miss Broadwood publish long and interesting notes on the song. Miss Gilchrist suggests that it is a degraded relic of a symbolical hymn in honour of the Virgin and in praise of the Heavenly Paradise, and Miss Broadwood agrees that 'mystical imagery lurks in it'. She further endeavours to prove from internal evidence that the scene of the song as it survives in modern times is laid in south Cornwall.

65 Down by a Riverside

References:
J.F.S.S. iii, p. 296, and iv, p. 281; SHARP Appalachian ii, 107; SHARP English County, p. 100. (LAWS, p. 257, P 18).

This song is not to be confused with 'The Bold Fisherman' which often appears under the title of 'Down by a Riverside'.
The tune is a close variant of 'The Banks of the Sweet Dundee'.

66 The Father in Ambush

References:
CREIGHTON Maritime Nova Scotia, p. 107; HUGHES Irish iv, p. 72; LEACH Labrador, 19; O LOCHLAINN Irish Street Ballads, 55; PEACOCK Newfoundland, p. 456.
I can offer no explanation of 'the discerning wall' in stanza 2.

NOTES ON THE SONGS

67 Johnny Doyle

References:
FLANDERS Green Mountain, p. 248; GARDNER Michigan, p. 69; HUDSON Mississippi, 44; HUGHES Irish iv, p. 72; J.F.S.S. v, p. 142; J. Irish F.S.S. i, p. 66; LEACH Labrador, 16; MACKENZIE Nova Scotia, 34; MORRIS Florida, 178; PEACOCK Newfoundland, p. 687; PETRIE Irish, 443; RANDOLPH Ozark i, 87; SHARP Appalachian ii, 83. (LAWS, p. 180, M 2).

Our text is somewhat confused and irregular, particularly stanzas 5 and 6. In SHARP Appalachian the equivalent of stanza 5 is:

> As soon as the minister he entered the door,
> My ear-bobs they bursted and fell to the floor,
> In sixty-five pieces my stay-laces flew;
> I thought in my soul my poor heart would break in two.

Some such incident is described in most versions. It is supposed to be an indication of great emotion.

68 There was a Lady in the East

References:
J.F.S.S. v, p. 139; PEACOCK Newfoundland, p. 126.

69 The Bonny Labouring Boy

References:
J.F.S.S. i, p. 206, and iii, p. 110; HUGHES Irish, p. 59; O LOCHLAINN Irish Street Ballads, 9; PEACOCK Newfoundland, 564. (LAWS, p. 187, M 14).
The words appear in ballad-sheets. In the complete version the girl takes flight and marries her bonny labouring boy.

70 On Board the Gallee

References:
CREIGHTON Maritime Nova Scotia, p. 43.

71 Young M'Tyre

I have found no other versions of this song.

72 The Rich Merchant's Daughter

Reference:
J.F.S.S. i, p. 50.

73 Bound Down to Derry

References:
CREIGHTON Traditional Nova Scotia, p. 179; LEACH Labrador, 33; PEACOCK Newfoundland, p. 582. (LAWS, p. 232, O 13).

74 Kind Fortune

This song was published with pf. accompaniment in KARPELES Newfoundland ii, 13. The only other versions I have come across are given without tune in Gavin Greig's *Folk Songs of the North-East* (Peterhead, Scotland, 1914, reprinted Folklore Associates, Hatboro, Pennsylvania, 1963) ii, art. clxxviii.

75 The Discharged Drummer

This has a somewhat similar theme to that of the last song. I do not know of any other version. It was published with pf. accompaniment in KARPELES Newfoundland i, 13.

76 Green Broom

References:
J.F.S.S. i, p. 84; SHARP English F.S. i, 33.
The words occur frequently in broadsides and are included in *Gammer Gurton's Garland*.

77 The Nightingale

References:
BELDEN Missouri, p. 239; BROWN N. Carolina iii and v, 13; EDDY Ohio, 103; J.F.S.S. viii, p. 194; PEACOCK Newfoundland, p. 594; RANDOLPH Ozark i, 58; SGARP Appalachian ii, 145. (LAWS, p. 255, P 14). I noted two other variants in Newfoundland.

78 Soldier, Will You Marry Me

References:
BROWN iii and v, 7; EDDY Ohio, 89; RANDOLPH Ozark i, 65;

NOTES ON THE SONGS

SHARP Appalachian ii, 90. Has been published with pf. accompaniment in KARPELES Newfoundland ii, 15.

We give only a few of the many references to this song, which is a great favourite on both sides of the Atlantic.

79 Young Men, Come Marry Me

Was published with pf. accompaniment in KARPELES Newfoundland i, 11. I know of no other version.

Mr. Ghaney described this as 'a very becoming song to sing in young company'.

80 The New Mown Hay

This song is somewhat similar to another which goes by the same title and is published by Bronson in Appendix A to 'The Baffled Knight' (ii, 1 and 2) but the dénouement is entirely different.

81 Go from My Window

Reference:
J.F.S.S. iii, p. 78.

There are many 'Go from My Window' songs, usually bearing the title 'Awake, Awake, [or Arise, Arise] you Drowsy Sleeper'. An extensive list is given in BELDEN Missouri, p. 118. The present song differs from the better-known type. J.F.S.S. gives two texts with tunes noted in Dorset. The texts are incomplete, but the stanzas given (two in the first version and five in the second) are practically the same as our text.

William Chappell in *Popular Music of the Olden Time* i, p. 140, refers to a number of sixteenth- and seventeenth-century versions, including Beaumont and Fletcher's 'Knight of the Burning Pestle'. The song is given in Johnson's *Scots Musical Museum* where it is described as 'An ancient ballad with its melody recovered by Burns'.

82 The Maiden's Lament

This song was published with pf. accompaniment in KARPELES Newfoundland i, 8.

It may be part of a longer song in which more detailed circumstances of the maiden's tragedy are related, but the tune is so essentially lyrical in character that it would not lend itself to the accompaniment of a long ballad.

Mr. Sullivan, an old man, had not sung the song for many years. He had studied it up for my special benefit as he thought I should appreciate it.

The rise of the sixth from the dominant at the beginning of the first phrase (and repeated in the second phrase) is very effective. Cf. PETRIE Irish, 128.

83 She's Like the Swallow

Two versions are given in PEACOCK Newfoundland, p. 711, both of which have the distinctive first stanza and include the line 'He has two hearts instead of one'. Peacock's version A is very close to our versions and although the singer learned the song from her mother, her comment that 'the air is just like that man sings on the radio' may mean that it has been influenced by the frequent broadcast performances which, I understand, the present version of the song enjoys. Another version is given in FOWKE Ontario, 57.

The present version was published with pf. accompaniment in KARPELES Newfoundland ii, 8.

An unpublished version noted by Cecil Sharp in Cambridgeshire finishes with the following stanzas:

> All down in the meadows away she goes
> To gather the flowers as they spring.
> She pluckèd red and she pluckèd blue
> Until she plucked her apron full.

> A flower for my pillow and one for my head,
> A green grass bolster for my bed;
> Then leaves that blow from tree to tree
> Shall be the coverlets over me.

> There is a man on yonder hill,
> He's got two hearts like iron and steel,
> He's got two hearts in the room of one,
> What a rogue he'll be when he's dead and gone.

This final stanza is as follows in a text noted by R. Vaughan Williams (J.F.S.S. ii, 1, p. 159):

> O yonder he stands on yonder hill,
> He's got a heart as hard as steel,

NOTES ON THE SONGS

He's gained two hearts in the room of one,
And he'll be a true lovier [lover] when I am gone.

84 Green Bushes

References:
CREIGHTON Songs Nova Scotia, 19; GREENLEAF Newfoundland, 30; J.F.S.S. v, p. 177, and viii, pp. 112 and 209; J. Irish F.S.S. i, p. 65; JOYCE Irish, 23; KIDSON, p. 47; SHARP Appalachian ii, 126; SHARP English i, 24 (LAWS, p. 249, P 2).

The singer did not remember the words of the song. A complete text is given in GREENLEAF.

There are interesting notes on the song (J.F.S.S. v, 177–80) by Miss Gilchrist and Miss Broadwood who show its connection with the song which appears in Buckstone's play of 'The Green Bushes' (1855) and the text of a 'Dialogue in imitation of Mr. H. Purcell—Between a Town Spark and a Country Lass' in Carey's *Musical Century* (1740).

85 The Cuckoo

References:
CREIGHTON Traditional Nova Scotia, p. 142; J.F.S.S. iii, p. 90, and vi, p. 14; RANDOLPH Ozark i, 49; SHARP Appalachian ii, 140; SHARP English F.S. i, 19. Has been published with pf. accompaniment in KARPELES Newfoundland ii, 11.

The tunes of this well-known song vary considerably. They are usually very beautiful as is the simple tune that we give here.

86 The Morning Dew

The singer could not remember any more words. I noted another version with a poor tune, which had a few additional rather confused lines.

The song is probably the same as JOYCE Irish, 416.

87 The Liar's Song

References:
LEACH Labrador, 111; PEACOCK Newfoundland, p. 25.

This is a type of nonsense song which is very popular among folk singers, cf. 'The Derby Ram' and 'Nottamun Town' (SHARP Appalachian ii, 141 and 191) and 'The Crocodile' (CREIGHTON Traditional Nova Scotia, p. 230, and BROADWOOD English County, p. 184). The last six bars of our tune are practically the same as those of 'The Crocodile'.

88 The Tree in the Wood

References:
CREIGHTON Songs Nova Scotia, 92; CREIGHTON Traditional Nova Scotia, p. 258; LEACH Labrador, 107; SHARP Appalachian ii, 206; SHARP English F.S. ii, 48. Has been published with pf. accompaniment in KARPELES Newfoundland i, 15.

This song is popular not only in North America and the British Isles but in many other European countries.
Like 'The Twelve Apostles' which follows, it is a cumulative song.

89 The Twelve Apostles

References:
BROWN N. Carolina ii and iv, 50; BROADWOOD English County, 154 and 156; GREENLEAF, 41 (no tune); J.F.S.S. vi, p. 24; PEACOCK Newfoundland, pp. 785 and 800; RANDOLPH Ozark iv, 605; SHARP Appalachian ii, 207; SHARP English F.S. ii, 47.

This song, as Miss Broadwood has truly remarked, demands a volume in itself. Since it is impossible to treat the subject adequately here, or even to give complete references to the many dissertations that have been written on the history and significance of the song, or to the attempts that have been made to explain the corrupt words which occur in it, the reader is advised to consult in the first place BROADWOOD, and SHARP English F.S., using the notes given in these publications as a point of departure for further research. Briefly, it may be said that the song is widely distributed and is known among Jewish as well as Christian communities. It should, strictly speaking, be sung as a cumulative song on the model of No. 88.

BIBLIOGRAPHY[1]

With key to abbreviations used
in the Notes on the Songs

ASHTON Street Ballads: John Ashton, *Modern Street Ballads*, London, 1888.

BARRY Maine: Phillips Barry, Fanny Hardy Eckstorm and Mary Winslow Smyth, *British Ballads from Maine*, Yale University Press, 1923.

BELDEN Missouri: H. M. Belden, *Ballads and Sea Songs*, Collected by the Missouri Folk-Lore Society, University of Missouri Studies, 1955 [1940].

⋊ BROADWOOD English County: Lucy E. Broadwood and J. A. Fuller Maitland, *English County Songs*, London, 1893.

BROADWOOD English Traditional: Lucy E. Broadwood, *English Traditional Songs and Carols*, London, 1908.

BRONSON: Bertrand Harris Bronson, *The Traditional Tunes of the Child Ballads with their Texts according to the extant records of Great Britain and America*, vol. i, Ballads 1 to 53; vol. ii, Ballads 54 to 113; vol. iii, Ballads 114 to 243. Princeton University Press, 1959 and 1962.[2]

BROWN N. Carolina: Frank C. Brown, *Collection of North Carolina Folklore*, General Editor, Ivey Newman White, vol. ii, *Folk Ballads from North Carolina* (1952); vol. iii, *Folk Songs from North Carolina* (1952); vol. iv, *The Music of the Ballads* (1957); vol. v, *The Music of the Songs* (1962). Vols. ii and iii, ed. Henry M. Belden and Arthur Palmer Hudson; vols. iv and v, ed. Jan Philip Schinhan. Duke University Press, N. Carolina.

BULLETIN of Northeast: *Bulletin of the Folksong Society of the Northeast*, 7 nos., reprinted by the American Folklore Society, Philadelphia, 1960.

CHILD: Francis James Child, *The English and Scottish Popular Ballads*, 5 vols., 10 parts, Boston 1882–98. Facsimile Edition, Dover Publications, New York, 1965.

COFFIN: Tristram P. Coffin, *The British Traditional Ballad in North America*, The American Folklore Society, Philadelphia, 1963 (revised edition).

(A critical bibliographical study of the texts of the 'Child' ballads —for references.)

[1] This is a list of publications to which reference is made in the Notes on the Songs. It is not intended to be a complete bibliography.
[2] The Roman numerals given in the Notes on the Songs indicate the number of the volume. Further volumes, which will complete the CHILD series, are in preparation.

BIBLIOGRAPHY

CREIGHTON Maritime Nova Scotia: Helen Creighton, *Maritime Folk Songs*, Toronto, 1962.

CREIGHTON Songs Nova Scotia: Helen Creighton, *Songs and Ballads from Nova Scotia*, Toronto, 1933.

CREIGHTON Traditional Nova Scotia: Helen Creighton and Doreen H. Senior, *Traditional Songs from Nova Scotia*, Toronto, 1950.

DAVIS Virginia: Arthur Kyle Davis Jr., *More Traditional Ballads of Virginia*, University of North Carolina Press, Chapel Hill, 1960.

EDDY Ohio: Mary O. Eddy, *Ballads and Songs from Ohio*, New York, 1939.

FLANDERS Green Mountain: Helen Hartness Flanders, *The New Green Mountain Songster*, Yale University Press, 1939.

FLANDERS New England: Helen Hartness Flanders, *Ancient Ballads Traditionally sung in New England*, 3 vols., University of Pennsylvania Press and Oxford University Press, 1960, 1961 and 1963.

FOWKE Ontario: Edith Fowke, *Traditional Singers and Songs from Ontario*, Folklore Associates, Hatboro, Penn., 1965.

GARDNER Michigan: Emelyn Elizabeth Gardner and Geraldine Jencks Chickering, *Ballads and Songs of Southern Michigan*, University of Michigan Press, 1939.

GREENLEAF Newfoundland: Elisabeth Bristol Greenleaf and Yarrow Mansfield, *Ballads and Sea Songs of Newfoundland*, Harvard University Press, 1933.

GREIG Aberdeen: Gavin Grieg and Alexander Keith, *Last Leaves of Traditional Ballads and Ballad Airs*, Aberdeen, 1925.

HUDSON Mississippi: Arthur Palmer Hudson, *Folk Songs of Mississippi*, University of North Carolina Press, 1936. (Text and notes—no tunes.)

HUGHES Irish: Herbert Hughes, *Irish Country Songs*, 4 vols., London, 1904–35.

J.E.F.D.S.S.: *Journal of the English Folk Dance and Song Society*, London, 1932. *In progress.*

J.F.S.S.: *Journal of the Folk-Song Society*, 8 vols., London, 1889–1931. (Note: Roman figures given in the Notes refer to volumes and not to parts.)

J. Irish F.S.S.: *Journal of the Irish Folk Song Society*, 29 vols., London and Dublin, 1904–39. Vol. xv (1919): *Traditional Folk Songs from Galway and Mayo*, coll. and ed. Mrs. Costello, Tuam. Vols. xxii–xxix (1927–39): *The Bunting Collection*, 6 parts, ed. D. J. O'Sullivan.

JOYCE Irish: P. W. Joyce, *Old Irish Folk Music and Songs*, London and Dublin, 1909.

KARPELES Newfoundland: Maud Karpeles, *Folk Songs from Newfoundland*, 2 vols., Oxford University Press, 1934.

NOTES ON THE SONGS

KIDSON: Frank Kidson, *Traditional Tunes*, Oxford, 1891.

LAWS: G. Malcolm Laws Jr., *American Balladry from British Broadsides*, American Folklore Society, Philadelphia, 1957. (A bibliographical syllabus—for references.)

LEACH Labrador: MacEdward Leach, *Folk Ballads and Songs of the Lower Labrador Coast*, National Museum of Canada, 1965.

MACKENZIE Nova Scotia: W. Roy Mackenzie, *Ballads and Sea Songs from Nova Scotia*, Harvard University Press, 1928.

MORRIS Florida: Alton C. Morris, *Folk Songs of Florida*, University of Florida Press, 1950.

O LOCHLAINN Irish Street Ballads: Colm O Lochlainn, *Irish Street Ballads*, Dublin and London, 1939.

PEACOCK Newfoundland: Kenneth Peacock, *Songs of the Newfoundland Outports*, National Museum of Canada, 1965.

PETRIE Irish: George Petrie, *The Complete Collection of Irish Music*, ed. Charles Villiers Stanford, 3 vols., London, 1905.

RANDOLPH Ozark: Vance Randolph, *Ozark Folk Songs*, 4 vols., Columbia, Missouri, 1946–50.

SHARP Appalachian: Cecil J. Sharp and Maud Karpeles, *English Folk Songs from the Southern Appalachians*, Oxford University Press, [1932] 1960.

SHARP English County: Cecil J. Sharp, *English County Folk-Songs*, London, 1961 (originally *Folk-Songs of England*, ed. Cecil J. Sharp in 5 vols., 1908–12); i H. E. D. Hammond, *Dorset*, pp. 1–39; ii R. Vaughan Williams, *The Eastern Counties*, pp. 40–94; iii George B. Gardiner, *Hampshire*, pp. 95–140; iv Cecil J. Sharp, *Various Counties*, pp. 141–80; v W. Percy Merrick, *Sussex*, pp. 181–223. (The pagination refers to the one-volume 1961 edition.)

SHARP English F.S.: Cecil J. Sharp, *English Folk Songs*, 2 vols., 1920. Selected edition, reprinted as Centenary Edition in 1 vol., London, 1959. (Also *One Hundred English Folksongs*, Boston, 1916.)

SHARP Somerset: Cecil J. Sharp, 5 vols. (vols. i to iii with Charles E. Marson), London and Taunton, 1904–9. (Most of the songs are included in *English Folk Songs*.)

APPENDIX

TEXTS ADAPTED FOR SINGING

1 THE OUTLANDISH KNIGHT
(Lady Isabel and the Elf Knight)

Give me some of your dada's gold
And some of your mamma's fee
And the very best nag in your father's barn
Where there lies thirty and three.

She gave him some of her dada's gold
And some of her mamma's fee
And the very best nag in her father's barn
Where there lies thirty and three.

She mounted on her milk-white steed
And he on the dapple grey;
They rode till they came to the salt sea side,
Three hours before it was day.

Light off, light off your milk-white steed,
Deliver it up unto me,
For six fair maids I have a-drowned here
And you the seventh shall be.

Take off your rich, your costly robe
And lay it down by me,
For it is too rich and too costly
To rot all in the salt sea.

O turn, O turn, young Willie, she says,
O turn your back to me,
For it is not fitting that such a ruffian
A naked woman should see.

He turned around his back to her
And his face to the leaves of the tree.
Pretty Polly she took him all into her arms
And throwed him into the sea.

Lie there, lie there, false Willie, she says,
Lie there instead of me.
For six fair maids you have a-drowned here;
The seventh have drownèd thee.

APPENDIX

She mounted on her milk-white steed
And led the dapple grey;
She rode till she came to her father's house
Three hours before it was day.

She rode till she came to her father's hall.
She heard what the parrot did say:
O where were you, my pretty Polly
This livelong summer's day?

Her father was up in his bedroom so high
And heard what the parrot did say.
What ails thee, what ails thee, my pretty parrot,
You prattle so long before day?

It's no laughing matter, the parrot did say,
That loudly I call unto thee;
For the cat has a-got in the window so high.
I fear that she will have me.

Well turned, well turned, my pretty parrot,
Well turned, well turned for me.
Thy cage shall be made of the glittering gold
And the doors of the best ivory.

The text has been amplified by several lines from versions noted by
Cecil Sharp in Somerset.

4B HIND HORN
OR
THE BEGGAR MAN

On board of the ship and away sailed he,
He sailed right away to a far countree.
He looked at his ring, it was pale and dim;
That showed that his love was false to him.

On board of the ship and back sailed he,
He sailed right back to his own countree;
He rode and he rode and he rode up the street;
An old beggar man he chanced to meet.

What news, what news, my old beggar man,
What news, what news by sea or land?
Tomorrow's your true love's wedding day,
And the Squire is invited to give her away.

O you put on my driving suit,
And I'll put on your begging rig.
Your driving suit it won't fit me,
My begging rig it won't fit thee.

But let it be right or let it be wrong,
The begging rig he did put on.
He rode till he came to Napoleon's gate,
And he lay on his staff in a weary state.

He saw his true love come tripping down the stairs,
Gold rings on her fingers and gold in her hair,
And in her hand a glass of wine,
All for to treat the old beggar man.

He drank and he drank and he drank so free,
And into the glass the ring slipped he.
Did you get it from land, did you get it from strand,
Did you get it from a drowned man's hand?

I neither got it from land or strand,
Nor neither from a drowned man's hand.
I got it from a true love courting me so gay,
And now I'll return it on her wedding day.

Then rings from her fingers she pulled off
And gold from her hair she did shake off.
I'll follow my true love for ever, ever more,
And beg my bread from door to door.

Between the kitchen and the hall
The old beggar suit he did let fall;
Her own true love, the flower of them all,
The best little fellow that stands in the hall.

In this composite version text A has been collated with the text which accompanies tune B.

5A THE CRUEL MOTHER

O there was a lady lived in New York,
  Fair flowers the valley O,
She was courted by her father's clerk
  Down by the greenwood sidey O.

She laid her back against a thorn,
And there she had two pretty babes born.

She had a knife both long and sharp,
She pierced it in the two babes' hearts.

She dug a grave both long and deep,
And she put those two pretty babes to sleep.

As she was walking her father's hall,
She saw two babes a-playing ball.

She said: Dear babes, if you were mine,
I would dress you up in silk so fine.

They said: Dear mother, when we were thine,
You neither dressed us coarse nor fine.

You took your apron wide and deep,
And you wrapped it around for a winding-sheet.

She said: Dear babes, it's you can tell,
If my poor soul is for heav'n or for hell.

O yes, dear mother, we can tell,
Whether your poor soul is for heav'n or for hell.

You have seven years to roll a stone,
  Seven more to stand alone,
And the rest of your time you'll walk alone
  Down by the greenwood sidey O.

You have seven more to ring a bell,
  Yes, dear mother, we can tell,
And it's seven more you'll spend in hell
  Down by the greenwood sidey O.

Composite version collated from various texts noted in Newfoundland.

Lady Margaret was sitting in her lonely bower,
'Twas built of lime and stone.
Lady Margaret was sitting in her lonely bower
And she heard a dismal moan.

O is it my father, the king, she cries,
Or is it my brother John?
Or is it my true love, Knight William, she cries,
From Scotland he has come?

It's not your father, the king, he cries,
Nor yet your brother John,
But it is your true love, Knight William, he cries,
From Scotland he has come.

Do you bring to me any apparel, she said,
Do you bring to me a ring?
Do you bring to me any token at all
That a true love ought to bring?

I've brought to you no apparel, he said,
I've brought to you no ring;
I've brought to you a white holland sheet
That my poor body lies in.

There's one request I'll ask of thee,
I hope you will grant it to me.
That is my faith and a troth, he said,
I left in pledge with thee.

Your faith and a troth I'll not bring to you,
Nor any such a thing,
Until you take me to yonder church
And wed me with a ring.

O God forbid, Lady Margaret, he said,
That ever that should be,
That the dead should arise and marry the quick
And vanish away from thee.

O she took hold of his white holland sheet
And tied it around her tight;

SWEET WILLIAM'S GHOST

And it's over the hills of a cold winter's night
In a dead man's company.

They walked till they came to the old churchyard
Where the graves were mossy green.
There is my home, Lady Margaret, he said,
And the place I do dwell in.

Is there any room at your head, she cried,
Or any at your feet,
Or any at your right-hand side
Where I can lie and sleep?

There is no room at my head, he cried,
Nor any at my feet,
There is no room at my right-hand side
For a lady to lie and sleep.

She took her hand all from her side
And struck him all on the breast.
Here is my faith and a troth, Knight William,
God grant your soul to rest.

The text has been collated with other versions collected in Newfoundland. The penultimate stanza accords with the usual printed
versions. In Newfoundland the following words were normally sung:

My father's at my head, he cried,
My mother's at my feet,
And there's three hell-hounds at my right side
That torment me from my sleep.

And one is for my drunkenness,
The other for my pride,
And the other's for deluding a fair pretty maid
And staying out late by night.

11A MATTHY GROVES
(*Little Musgrave*)

'Twas on one day and a high holiday,
The best day of the year,
Young Matthy Groves went to the church
Some holy words to hear, hear,
Some holy words to hear.

Some were dressed in robes of satin
And more were dressed in silk;
And who should come in but Lord Allen's wife
And her skin as white as milk.

She lookèd up and she lookèd down,
Young Matthy Groves did spy.
Come home with me this very night
In bed with me to lie.

I will not nor I cannot come,
I would not for my life,
For by the ring that's on your finger
You are Lord Allen's wife.

And if I am Lord Allen's wife,
O what is that to thee?
For Lord Allen is gone to Newcast-el
King Henry for to see.

The little foot-page was standing by,
He took to his heels and ran
And when he got to the riverside
He fell to his breast and swam.

He swam till he came to King Henry's door
And he knocked so loud at the ring.
And no one so ready as Lord Allen himself
For to let that foot-page in.

What news, what news, my little foot-page,
What news has thou brought me?
Bad news, bad news and very bad news,
The worst of news to thee.

MATTHY GROVES

Is any of my castles fallen down,
Or any of my towers won,
Or is my fair lady put to bed
With a daughter or a son?

There's none of your castles fallen down,
Nor none of your towers won,
But this very night young Matthy Groves
In bed with your lady's come.

He callèd up all his merry men
And placed them in a row,
He ordered them not to speak one word
Nor neither a horn to blow.

But one of Lord Allen's merry men
To gain his mistress's will,
He put a horn all to his mouth
And he blew both loud and shrill.

I thought I heard Lord Allen's voice,
I thought I heard him say:
A man that's in bed with another man's wife,
'Tis time to be jogging away.

Come huddle me, come cuddle me
And shelter me from the cold;
It's only my father's shepherd boy
A-driving his sheep to fold.

He huddled her, he cuddled her,
Till they both fell fast-asleep
And early next morn when they awoke
Lord Allen stood at their feet.

O how do you like my bed, he said,
And how do you like my sheet
And how do you like my fair lady
Lies in your arms to sleep?

Very well I like your bed, he said,
And better I like your sheet,
But the best of all is your gay lady
That lies in my arms asleep.

Arise, arise, young Matthy Groves,
And some of your clothes put on.
It ne'er shall be said when I am dead,
I killed a naked man.

I would not nor I cannot rise,
Nor I would not for my life,
For you have got two swords by your side
And I've got ne'er a knife.

If I have two swords by my side,
I paid for them in my purse;
Then you can take the best of them
And I will take the worst.

The very first stroke young Matthy made,
He wounded Lord Allen sore;
The very next stroke Lord Allen made,
Young Groves he struck no more.

He callèd up his fair lady
And daddled her on his knee,
Saying: Choose, O choose, my fair lady,
Between young Groves and me.

Very well I like your lips,
Very well I like your chin
But better I like young Matthy Groves
Than you and all your kin.

The bells did ring, the birds did sing,
The bells did toll for sorrow.
Lord Allen killed his wife today
And he'll be hanged tomorrow.

This is mainly version B with a few verbal alterations and some lines from version A. Both versions omit the stanza describing Lord Allen's killing of his wife.

The following stanza, noted in North Carolina, can if desired, be interpolated before the final stanza:

He took her by the lily-white hand,
He led her through the hall;
He drew his sword, cut off her head
And kicked it against the wall.

13B LAMKIN

Said the lord to his lady
As he was going away,
Beware of proud Lamkin,
For he comes up this way.
What do I care for Lamkin,
Or for any of his kin,
When my doors are well bolted
And my windows barred in?

He was scarce gone one hour,
When proud Lamkin came in.
He knocked at the hall door
And the nurse let him in.
O where is your master?
Is he not within?
He's gone to old England
Cried the false nurse to him.

O where is your mistress?
Is she not within?
She's up in her chamber
With the windows barred in.
How am I to get at her?
Proud Lamkin did cry.
O here is young Sir Johnson,
Pierce him and he'll cry.

O mistress, dearest mistress,
How can you sleep so fast?
Can't you hear your young Sir Johnson
A-crying his last?
I can't pacify him
On the nurse-milk or pap,
I pray you to come down,
Quiet him on your lap.

How can I come downstairs
On a cold winter's night,
No spark of fire burning,
No candle alight.
You've got two white holland sheets
As white as the snow,

I pray you come down
By the light of them so.

As she was coming downstairs
Not thinking much harm,
Proud Lamkin awaited,
Took her by the arm.
I have got you, I have got you,
Proud Lamkin did cry,
For years I have waited,
But I've got you at last.

O spare my life, Lamkin,
Till one, two o'clock,
And I'll give you all the money
You can carry on your back.
If you'll give me the money
Like the sand in the sea,
I will not keep my bright sword
From your white skin so free.

O spare my life, Lamkin,
For one half an hour,
I'll give you my daughter Betsy,
Although she's my flower.
O where is your daughter?
Go send her to me;
She can hold the silver basin
While your heart's blood runs free.

There was blood in the nursery
And blood in the hall,
And blood on the staircase,
And her heart's blood over all.
Proud Lamkin was taken
To the gallows to die
And the false nurse was burnèd
In a fire near by.

This tune is mainly text A, but it is suggested that it should be sung to tune B. A few stanzas have been omitted in order to fit the text to the eight-line stanza. In a fragment of the text also noted in Newfoundland, Pretty Betsy and not the nurse is offered to Lamkin and this substitution has been made here. It is the more usual form.

14A WILLIE o' WINSBURY

There was a lady fair in the north country,
And she dressèd all in green.
As she was a-sitting in her father's castle,
She saw a ship sail in. [*bis*]

O daughter, dear daughter, the father he cried,
What makes you look so pale and wan,
Or have you had any heavy sickness,
Or in love with some young man?

O father, dear father, the daughter she said,
If I do look so pale and wan,
I've had no heavy sickness,
I'm in love with some young man.

O is he a duke or a squire, he said,
Or a man of a high degree,
Or is he one of my humble sailor boys
That ploughs o'er the raging sea?

O he is not a duke nor a squire, she says,
Nor a man of a high degree,
But he is one of your humble sailor boys
That ploughs o'er the raging sea.

Now daughter, dear daughter, the father he says,
If it's true what you're telling me,
Tomorrow morning at eight o'clock
It's hangèd your love will be.

O father, dear father, the daughter she cries,
If it's true what you're telling me,
If tomorrow morning my love shall be hanged,
You will get no good of me.

Now the king called down his merry, merry men,
By one, by two, by three,
Fair Willie was always the first that came down,
But now the last was he.

O Willie came down all step after step,

309

All dressed in a suit of silk,
With his two cherry cheeks and his curly brown hair
And his skin as white as milk.

O daughter, dear daughter, the father he cries,
I will lay no blame to thee;
For if I was a woman instead of a man,
I would die for love of him.

O you can marry my daughter, he cries,
You can take her by the hand,
And you can come and dine with me
And be head over all my land.

Yes, I will marry your daughter, he says,
I will take her by the hand,
And I will go and dine with you,
But to hell with all your land.

Where you can give her one guinea,
I can give her thirty-three,
Although I am one of your humble sailor boys
That ploughs o'er the raging sea.

Composite text collated from various versions noted in Newfoundland.

If the above text is sung to other versions of the tune the words 'pale and' in the second and third stanzas will have to be omitted.

15 THE BAILIFF'S DAUGHTER
OF ISLINGTON

It's of a youth and a well-belovèd youth,
It's of a squire's son,
And he courted Bailey's own daughter dear
As she lived in sweet Islinkington.[1]

And when his parents came to know
They had such a silly son,
They sent him away to fair London Town
And a prentice had him bound.

One day all in the summer-time
The girls went out to play,
All but the Bailey's daughter dear,
So cunningly she stole away.

And she pulled off her gown of green
And dressed in ragged attire
And went away to fair London Town
Her true love to enquire.

She travelled on one livelong year,
One livelong year and a day;
And who did she meet but her own true love
As he came riding that way.

As she was going up the street
And he came riding down,
She took his horse all by the bridle side
And she swung herself right round.

O where are you going, my fair pretty maid?
And where are you going? cried she.
I am in search of the Bailey's daughter dear
As she lived in sweet Islinkington.

The Bailey's daughter of Islinkington,
She's dead and don't you know,
The Bailey's daughter of Islinkington,
She's been dead, sir, this long time ago.

[1] Islington or Islington town.

If Bailey's daughter is now dead,
I'll sell my milk-white steed;
And I'll go to some foreign country
Where no man shall never, never know.

The Bailey's daughter is not dead,
She still remains alive;
And here she is all by the bridle side
All ready for to be your bride.

O farewell grief and sorrow too,
Ten thousand joys or more,
For now I have got my heart's delight,
The girl that I adore.

Stanzas 2–5 and 11 have been taken from English versions collected by Cecil Sharp.

17A THE GYPSY LADDIE

Seven gypsies stood in a row,
They sang so sweetly through the air,
And they sang so sweet and so very, very sweet,
They charmed the heart of a lady fair.

She was sitting in her castle high,
Smiling on those gypsies O;
Some jealous thought came into her mind,
She would follow the dark-eyed gypsies O.

When the lord came home that night,
Enquiring for his lady O,
I'm afraid, I'm afraid, says the old kitchen maid,
That she followed the dark-eyed gypsies O.

Saddle my horse, come saddle my team,
And brace my pistols by my side
That I may ride till broad daylight
And follow the dark-eyed gypsy O.

He rode West and then rode North
Till he came to a farmer's door.
O farmer, farmer, tell me the truth,
Have you seen the dark-eyed gypsies O?

You ride on, the old farmer cried,
Down in yonder valley O,
And there you'll find your own true love
In the arms of a dark-eyed gypsy O.

Last night you lay on your feather bed
With blankets round you white as snow,
And tonight you lie on the cold damp ground
In the arms of a dark-eyed gypsy O.

Will you come home, my fair lady,
Will you come home, my honey O,
Or will you forsake your own native land
And follow the dark-eyed gypsy O?

I'll forsake my castle, she said,
And I'll forsake my native land.
I'll eat of the grass and drink of the dew
And follow the dark-eyed gypsy O.

Composite version collated from various texts noted in Newfoundland.

19 THE DOWIE DENS OF YARROW
(*The Braes o' Yarrow*)

There was a squire lived in the town,
He had one daughter Sarah.
She admired her father's clerk,
The ploughboy John from Yarrow.

As he was going up the lane,
The lane so very narrow,
There he espied nine hired men
Come to fight with him in Yarrow.

Three withdrew and three he slew
And three lay deadly wounded
And her brother he stepped up behind
To pierce him bodily under.

Go home, go home, you false young man
And tell your sister Sarah
That the prettiest flower that bloomed in June
Is the man who died in Yarrow.

She said: Brother dear, I had a dream,
It caused me fear and sorrow.
I dreamed that I was gathering flowers
In the dewy dales of Yarrow.

O sister dear, I can read your dream
That caused you fear and sorrow.
The sweetest flower that bloomed in June
Is the man who died in Yarrow.

As she went over yon high hill
And down yon dale so narrow,
'Twas there she saw her true love John
A-bleeding sore in Yarrow.

She washed his face, she combed his hair,
As she had done before O;
She kissed the blood from off his wounds
In the dewy dales of Yarrow.

Her hair it was three-quarters long,
Its colour it was yellow;
She tied it round his middle so small
And she carried him home to Yarrow.

Her father spoke to her one day:
What need for all this sorrow?
I'll wed you to a better man
Than the one you lost in Yarrow.

O father dear, you have seven sons.
You may wed them all tomorrow.
But a prettier flower ne'er bloomed in June
Than the one I lost in Yarrow.

The last six stanzas have been adapted from Gavin Greig's *Last Leaves of Traditional Ballads and Ballad Airs*, pp. 142–3.

21A THE LOVER'S GHOST
(*The Grey Cock*)

O Johnny he promised to marry me.
I fear he's with some fair one gone.
And there's something that bewails him, I don't know what it is,
And I'm weary from lying alone.

John he came there at the hour appointed;
He tapped at the window so low.
This fair maid arose and she hurried on her clothes,
And welcomed her true love home.

She took him by the hand and laid him down;
She felt he was colder than clay.
She said: My dearest dear, if I only had my wish
This long night would never be day.

Crow up, crow up, my little bird,
And don't you crow before day,
And your cage shall be made of the glittering gold, she says,
And your doors of the silver so gay.

Where is your soft bed of down, my love,
And where is your white holland sheet,
And where is the fair maid that watches on you
While you are taking your long silent sleep?

The sand is my soft bed of down, my love,
The sea is my white holland sheet,
And long hungry worms will feed off of me
While I sleep every night in the deep.

O when will I see you, my love, she cries,
And when will I see you again?
When the little fishes fly and the seas they do run dry
And the hard rocks they melt with the sun.

The text with some verbal alterations has been supplemented by
others noted in Newfoundland.

Text C, which is the most complete, can be sung to all three versions of the tune. If sung to tune A, the last three syllables of the third line will have to be repeated.

25 THE BLOODY GARDENER

For the sake of clarity the following lines are offered as an alternative to lines 3 and 4 of the first stanza:

But his mother laid a snare and false letters she did write,
Saying: Meet me in the garden here this night.

The scansion of the fourth line of the penultimate stanza would be better if the words 'shook her head' were omitted.

26 SHOOTING OF HIS DEAR

It is not clear from the text that it is the dead girl's ghost that is speaking. We therefore suggest that the last two stanzas should be substituted by the following lines:

On the day of her trial her ghost did appear
Saying: Randal, Jimmy Randal, Jimmy Randal go clear.

My apron flew around me, he took me for a swan,
He shot me and killed me. My name is Molly Bond.

28B THE SEA CAPTAIN
OR
THE MAID ON THE SHORE

It's of a sea captain that ploughs the salt sea,
The seas were fine, calm and clear O.
A beautiful damsel he chanced for to spy,
A-walking alone on the shore, shore,
A-walking alone on the shore.

O what will I give to my sailors so bold?
Ten guineas I vow and declare O,
If you'll fetch me that lady on board of my ship
That walks all alone on the shore, shore,
That walks all alone on the shore.

The sailors did hoist out a very long boat
And straight for the shore they did steer O,
Saying: Ma'am, if you please, will you enter on board,
And view a fine cargo of ware, ware,
And view a fine cargo of ware?

With long persuading they got her on board,
The seas they were fine, calm and clear O.
She sat herself down in the stern of the boat
And straight for the ship they did steer, steer,
And straight for the ship they did steer.

And when they arrived alongside of the ship
The captain he ordered a chair O,
Saying: First you shall lie in my arms all this night
And the next you shall marry me, dear, dear,
And the next you shall marry me, dear.

She set herself down in the stern of the ship,
The seas they were fine, calm and clear O.
She sang so neat, so sweet and complete,
She sang sailors and captain to sleep, sleep,
She sang sailors and captain to sleep.

She robbed them of silver, she robbed them of gold,
She robbed them of costly ware O.

The captain's broadsword she took for an oar,
And she paddled away for the shore, shore,
And she paddled away for the shore.

When the captain awoke and he found she was gone
He was like a man in despair O.
He called up his men and commanded a boat
To row him away for the shore, shore,
To row him away for the shore.

He lowered himself down in the stern of the boat,
And away for the shore they did steer O.
She saluted the captain as well as the crew,
Saying: I'm a maiden once more on the shore, shore,
I'm a maiden once more on the shore.

Composite version collated from various Newfoundland texts. If sung to tune A, it will be necessary to omit the final 'O' in the second line of each stanza.

32 EDWIN IN THE LOWLANDS LOW
OR
YOUNG EDMUND

The six-line stanza (No. 7) might be replaced by the following two stanzas:

Young Amy rose, put on her clothes
And to her parents did go,
Saying: Where's the man came here last night
That ploughs the lowlands low.

O daughter, dearest daughter,
There's no one here must know
But he is dead, no tales he'll tell;
He lies in the lowlands low.

O Nancy, lovely Nancy, I'm going for to leave you,
Down to the East Indies, I'm bound for to steer,
And it's by my long absence, lovely Nancy, don't grieve you,
For I will be back in the Spring of the year.

I'll dress as a sailor and with you I'll wander,
In the midst of all danger with you I shan't fail,
In the cold stormy weather when the hurricane's blowing,
My dear, I'll be ready to reef your topsail.

Your dear little fingers our cables can't handle,
Your neat little feet, love, to the main-top can't go,
Your delicate body cold winds can't endure.
I advise you, lovely Nancy, to the seas do not go.

Come all you young maidens by me take a warning,
Don't never love a sailor that sails o'er the main,
For today they will court you and tomorrow they'll slight you,
And they'll leave you in sorrow and grief to complain.

Composite text collated from A and B.

54 THE WINTER'S GONE AND PAST

The last three stanzas of the text are somewhat confused, and singers may therefore wish to confine themselves to the first three stanzas, or else to substitute some of the lines of the broadside text given in the Notes.

57A THE BLIND BEGGAR'S DAUGHTER
OF BETHNAL GREEN

In version A, reference to the beggar's daughter is missing in the first stanza. It is therefore suggested that the following, which has been combined with other versions, should replace stanza 1.

It was of a blind beggar from Bethlehem Tyne,
He had but one daughter, she was comely and fine,
She was neat, tall and handsome in every degree,
And every one called her their bonny Betsy.

64A THE STREAMS OF LOVELY NANCY
OR
THE DREAMS OF LOVELY NANCY

The streams of lovely Nancy divide in three parts,
Where young men and maidens go to seek their sweethearts.
It's drinking strong liquor makes my poor heart ache;
The noise in yonder valley caused the rocks for to break.

As a sailor and his true love were walking along,
Said the sailor to his true love: I will sing you a song.
It's a false-hearted woman causes me for to say:
Fare you well, my lovely Nancy, I'm now bound away.

I will go to yonder mountain where the wild fowl does fly;
There is one bird among them, she flies very high.
If I had her in my arms but one moment to stand,
You would see how I'd tame her by the sleight of my hand.

I will go to yonder mountain where the castle does stand,
It's built up with ivory all on the dark strand,
It's built up with ivory and diamonds so bright;
It's a signal for sailors on a dark stormy night.

The bright star of Erion so beautiful does shine,
With her hair o'er her shoulder like amber so brown,
I delight in her company more than gold I declare,
Although she does slight me, she's the girl I love dear.

Shortened composite version collated from various Newfoundland
texts.

It is suggested that the last stanza, which lacks two lines, should be omitted, or, if preferred, could be sung to the first, second and last lines of the melody.

In Bristol lived a damsel,
Her age was scarce sixteen,
And courted she was by many
Her favour for to win.

Till at length up stepped a drummer
And gave to her one kiss,
And said: Dear honoured lady,
In the regiment will you 'list?

O yes, replied the damsel,
And that I'll surely do,
For I do like your music,
Likewise your rat-tat-too.

But if you'll consent to marry
And to lie all by my side,
I will buy you your discharge, love,
In a carriage you will ride.

O yes, replied the drummer,
How happy should I be,
But I'm afraid that you won't wed
With a poor young man like me.

O that you may depend on,
The lady made reply,
For if I don't wed with you, young man,
I will never be made a bride.

This couple they got married,
And servants at their call.
And now he's knocked off playing
Among his comrades all.

Composite version collated from texts A and B.

It is suggested that the following lines, taken from an English text noted by Cecil Sharp, should be interpolated before the incomplete last stanza of the text:

> Then John he came back and upstairs he did go
> And he entered that fair lady's room, gay room,
> Dear Johnny, said she, O will you marry me?
> Will you marry that lady in bloom, in bloom,
> Will you marry that lady in bloom?
>
> Then John gave consent and to the church went
> And he married that lady in bloom in bloom.

82 THE MAIDEN'S LAMENT

As I roved out one evening in Spring
Down by a silent sweet shady grove,
I heard a maiden making sad lament,
She cried: Alas, I have lost my love.

O love is like an unquenching fire,
Like a raging fire it seems to burn.
Unto my cold grave I will retire,
Unto my friends I will ne'er return.

Come all you fair maids like me a-dying,
It's now I'm taking my last farewell.
And all you small birds round me flying,
Let your sweet notes be my passing bell.

This is an abridged version with the omission of the not very intelligible stanzas about the intervention of the hard-hearted parents.

83 SHE'S LIKE THE SWALLOW

She's like the swallow that flies so high,
She's like the river that never runs dry,
She's like the sunshine on the lee shore,
I love my love and love is no more.

'Twas out in the garden this fair maid did go,
A-picking the beautiful prim-e-rose;
The more she plucked the more she pulled
Until she got her a-per-on full.

It's out of those roses she made a bed,
A stony pillow for her head.
She laid her down, no word did say,
Until this fair maid's heart did break.

She's like the swallow that flies so high,
She's like the river that never runs dry,
She's like the sunshine on the lee shore,
I love my love and love is no more.

Stanza 3 of the original has been slightly amended and the repetition of stanza 1 is given in place of the last corrupt and incomplete lines.

85 THE CUCKOO

The cuckoo is a fine bird,
She sings as she flies,
And the more she sings Cuckoo
The more the summer draws nigh.

I wish I were a scholar
And could handle a pen;
I would write a private letter,
To my true love I would send.

I would send and let you know, my love,
Of my sorrow, grief and woe;
But my blessings attend you
Wherever you may go.

The cuckoo is a fine bird,
She sings as she flies,
And the more she sings Cuckoo
The summer draws nigh.

Stanza 3 is taken from an English version.

The pink, the lily and the blooming rose
Grow in the garden where my love goes;
The little small birds they do rejoice
When they think they hear my love Jimmy's voice.

O James Machree, I do love you well,
I love you better than tongue can tell;
There's not one drop of the morning dew
That's half so sweet as one kiss from you.

    The second stanza is a compilation of two lines taken from another version and the incomplete first stanza of the original.

In stanza 3 the extra line can be avoided by substituting the following for lines 3 and 4:

I bought myself a coal-black dog, his paws were nine miles wide,

INDEX OF TITLES

INDEX OF TITLES

339

INDEX OF TITLES